BESTSELLER

MASTERING PROMPT ENGINEERING UNLOCKING THE FULL POTENTIAL OF AI

JAGDISH KRISHANLAL ARORA

Mastering Prompt Engineering

Jagdish Krishanlal Arora

Published by Jagdish Krishanlal Arora, 2025.

Table of Contents

Also By Jagdish Krishanlal Arora

About the Author

Mastering Prompt Engineering: Unlocking the Full Potential of AI
By
Jagdish Krishanlal Arora
jagdishkarora@outlook.com

Chapter 1: Introduction to Prompt Engineering

- **Prompt engineering** is the process of designing effective inputs (prompts) to guide AI models in generating desired outputs.
- It is important because it ensures **accuracy, relevance, efficiency, and versatility** in AI-generated content.
- Key concepts include **prompts, context, instructions, output format, constraints, and examples**.

BY MASTERING THESE basics, you'll be well on your way to creating prompts that unlock the full potential of AI models. In the next chapter, we'll dive deeper into how AI models work and how to assess their capabilities.

1.1 What is Prompt Engineering?

Prompt engineering is the process of designing and refining inputs (called **prompts**) to guide AI models, particularly language models, in generating the desired outputs. It involves understanding how AI models interpret and respond to different types of inputs and using this knowledge to craft prompts that produce accurate, relevant, and useful results.

In simpler terms, prompt engineering is like giving clear and specific instructions to an AI so that it can provide the best possible answer or perform a task effectively. It's a blend of creativity and technical understanding, as you need to know how the AI "thinks" (or rather, predicts) to get the results you want.

1.2 Why is Prompt Engineering Important?

Prompt engineering is crucial because **the quality of the AI's output depends heavily on the quality of the input prompt**. Here's why it matters:

1. **Accuracy:** Well-crafted prompts help the AI generate more accurate and reliable responses.

2. **Relevance:** Prompts ensure that the AI stays on topic and provides information that is relevant to the task at hand.
3. **Efficiency:** Good prompts reduce the need for multiple iterations or corrections, saving time and resources.
4. **Versatility:** Prompt engineering allows AI models to be used in a wide range of applications, from customer service chatbots to complex data analysis and creative writing.

In short, **effective prompt engineering ensures that AI models perform at their best**, making them more useful and reliable in real-world applications.

1.3 Basic Concepts and Terminology

To get started with prompt engineering, it's important to understand some key terms and concepts:

1. **Prompt:**
   - The input given to an AI model to generate a response.
   - Example: *"Explain the concept of gravity in simple terms."*
2. **Context:**
   - Background information provided to the model to guide its response.
   - Example: *"You are a physics teacher explaining gravity to a 10-year-old student."*
3. **Instruction:**
   - The specific task or request given to the model.
   - Example: *"Write a short paragraph explaining gravity."*
4. **Output Format:**
   - The structure in which the model's response should be presented.
   - Example: *"Provide the explanation in bullet points."*
5. **Constraints:**
   - Limitations or requirements for the response.
   - Example: *"Keep the explanation under 100 words."*
6. **Examples:**
   - Demonstrations of desired input-output pairs to guide the model.

- o Example:
  - ▪ Input: *"Explain photosynthesis."*
  - ▪ Output: *"Photosynthesis is the process by which plants use sunlight to make food."*

Mathematical Examples and Reasoning

To further illustrate the power of prompt engineering, let's dive into **10 mathematical examples** that demonstrate how well-crafted prompts can guide AI models to solve problems step-by-step. These examples will include both the prompts and the AI-generated outputs.

Example 1: Basic Arithmetic
Prompt:
"Solve the following arithmetic problem step by step: 45 + 67 - 23."

AI Output:

1. First, add 45 and 67:
   $45 + 67 = 112$
2. Next, subtract 23 from the result:
   $112 - 23 = 89$
3. The final answer is **89**.

Example 2: Multiplication with Decimals
Prompt:
"Calculate the product of 12.5 and 3.4. Show each step of the calculation."

AI Output:

1. Multiply 12.5 by 3:
   $12.5 \times 3 = 37.5$
2. Multiply 12.5 by 0.4:
   $12.5 \times 0.4 = 5.0$
3. Add the two results together:
   $37.5 + 5.0 = 42.5$
4. The final answer is **42.5**.

Example 3: Division with Remainders
Prompt:

"Divide 127 by 8 and provide the quotient and remainder. Show your work."
AI Output:

1. Divide 127 by 8:
   8 goes into 127 a total of 15 times ($8 \times 15 = 120$).
2. Subtract 120 from 127 to find the remainder:
   $127 - 120 = 7$
3. The quotient is **15**, and the remainder is **7**.

Example 4: Solving Linear Equations
Prompt:
"Solve for x in the equation: 3x + 5 = 20. Show each step."
AI Output:

1. Subtract 5 from both sides of the equation:
   $3x + 5 - 5 = 20 - 5$
   $3x = 15$
2. Divide both sides by 3:
   $3x / 3 = 15 / 3$
   $x = 5$
3. The solution is **x = 5**.

Example 5: Quadratic Equation
Prompt:
"Solve the quadratic equation: x² - 5x + 6 = 0. Show the steps."
AI Output:

1. Factor the quadratic equation:
   $x^2 - 5x + 6 = (x - 2)(x - 3) = 0$
2. Set each factor equal to zero:
   $x - 2 = 0 \rightarrow x = 2$
   $x - 3 = 0 \rightarrow x = 3$
3. The solutions are **x = 2** and **x = 3**.

Example 6: Percentage Calculation
Prompt:
"What is 25% of 320? Show the calculation."
AI Output:

1. Convert 25% to a decimal:
   25% = 0.25
2. Multiply 0.25 by 320:
   0.25 × 320 = 80
3. The answer is **80**.

Example 7: Area of a Circle
Prompt:
"Calculate the area of a circle with a radius of 7 units. Use π = 3.14. Show the steps."
AI Output:

1. The formula for the area of a circle is:
   Area = $\pi \times r^2$
2. Substitute the radius (r = 7) and π = 3.14:
   Area = 3.14×7^2
3. Calculate 7^2:
   $7^2 = 49$
4. Multiply by π:
   3.14 × 49 = 153.86
5. The area is **153.86 square units**.

Example 8: Volume of a Cylinder
Prompt:
"Find the volume of a cylinder with a radius of 4 units and a height of 10 units. Use π = 3.14. Show the steps."
AI Output:

1. The formula for the volume of a cylinder is:
   Volume = $\pi \times r^2 \times h$
2. Substitute the radius (r = 4), height (h = 10), and π = 3.14:
   Volume = $3.14 \times 4^2 \times 10$
3. Calculate 4^2:
   $4^2 = 16$
4. Multiply by π and height:
   3.14 × 16 × 10 = 502.4
5. The volume is **502.4 cubic units**.

Example 9: Probability

Prompt:

"A bag contains 5 red marbles, 3 blue marbles, and 2 green marbles. What is the probability of drawing a red marble? Show the steps."

AI Output:

1. Calculate the total number of marbles:
   5 (red) + 3 (blue) + 2 (green) = 10 marbles
2. The probability of drawing a red marble is:
   Probability = Number of red marbles / Total marbles
   Probability = 5 / 10 = 0.5
3. The probability is **0.5** or **50%**.

Example 10: Compound Interest
Prompt:

"Calculate the compound interest on a principal of $1,000 at an annual interest rate of 5% compounded annually for 3 years. Show the steps."

AI Output:

1. The formula for compound interest is:
   $A = P \times (1 + r/n)^{(nt)}$
   Where:
   - A = Final amount
   - P = Principal ($1,000)
   - r = Annual interest rate (5% or 0.05)
   - n = Number of times interest is compounded per year (1)
   - t = Time in years (3)
2. Substitute the values into the formula:
   $A = 1000 \times (1 + 0.05/1)^{(1\times3)}$
   $A = 1000 \times (1.05)^3$
3. Calculate $(1.05)^3$:
   $(1.05)^3 = 1.157625$
4. Multiply by the principal:
   $A = 1000 \times 1.157625 = 1157.63$
5. The final amount after 3 years is **$1,157.63**.
6. The compound interest earned is:
   Interest = $A - P$ = 1157.63 - 1000 = **$157.63**.

Text-Based Examples and Reasoning

Now, let's explore **text-based examples** to demonstrate how prompt engineering can guide AI models to generate coherent and contextually appropriate responses.

Example 1: Summarization

Prompt:

"Summarize the following paragraph in one sentence: 'The Industrial Revolution, which began in the late 18th century, marked a major turning point in history. Almost every aspect of daily life was influenced in some way, particularly in the fields of manufacturing, transportation, and agriculture.'"

AI Output:

"The Industrial Revolution, starting in the late 18th century, significantly transformed daily life, especially in manufacturing, transportation, and agriculture."

Example 2: Paraphrasing

Prompt:

"Paraphrase the following sentence: 'The quick brown fox jumps over the lazy dog.'"

AI Output:

"A fast brown fox leaps over a sleepy dog."

Example 3: Creative Writing

Prompt:

"Write a short story about a robot who learns to paint. Use no more than 100 words."

AI Output:

"In a small workshop, a robot named Pixel discovered a box of paints. At first, its strokes were mechanical, but over time, it began to create vibrant landscapes. The other robots laughed, calling it a waste of energy. But Pixel didn't care. It painted sunsets, forests, and oceans, capturing emotions it couldn't feel. One day, a human saw Pixel's work and cried tears of joy. From that day on, Pixel became the first robot artist, proving that even without a heart, it could touch the soul."

Example 4: Explanation

Prompt:

"Explain the concept of blockchain in simple terms."

AI Output:

"Blockchain is like a digital ledger that records transactions in a secure and transparent way. Imagine a notebook where every page is linked to the previous one, and once something is written, it can't be erased or changed. This makes it very hard for anyone to cheat or alter the records. It's used in things like cryptocurrencies (e.g., Bitcoin) to keep track of who owns what."

Example 5: Role-Based Prompting
Prompt:
"You are a historian. Explain the causes of World War I in three bullet points."

AI Output:

- **Alliances:** European countries formed complex alliances, pulling multiple nations into conflict.
- **Militarism:** An arms race increased tensions and readiness for war.
- **Nationalism:** Intense national pride and territorial disputes fuelled hostilities.

Prompt engineering is a powerful tool for guiding AI models to produce accurate, relevant, and useful outputs. By understanding the basics of prompt design and applying structured techniques, you can unlock the full potential of AI in various applications, from solving mathematical problems to generating creative content. The examples provided in this chapter demonstrate how well-crafted prompts can lead to clear and effective AI-generated responses, whether for mathematical reasoning or text-based tasks. In the next chapter, we'll explore how AI models work and how to assess their capabilities in more detail.

Chapter 2: Understanding AI Models

ARTIFICIAL INTELLIGENCE (AI) models, particularly language models, have become integral to modern technology, powering everything from virtual assistants to content generation tools. Understanding how these models work, their strengths, limitations, and how to assess their capabilities is crucial for effectively leveraging them. This chapter delves into the mechanics of AI models, their potential, and their constraints, providing a comprehensive foundation for working with them.

2.1 How AI Models Work

AI models, especially language models, are designed to predict and generate text based on patterns learned from vast amounts of training data. These models operate by analysing input prompts and predicting the most likely sequence of words or tokens that should follow. Here's a breakdown of how they work:

Training Process

AI models are trained on large datasets containing text from diverse sources, such as books, articles, and websites. During training, the model learns statistical relationships between words, phrases, and sentences. For example, it learns that the word "cat" is often associated with "meow" or "purr," and that "Paris" is frequently mentioned alongside "France."

Tokenization

Text input is broken down into smaller units called tokens, which can be words, parts of words, or even characters. For instance, the sentence "AI is amazing" might be tokenized into ["AI", "is", "amazing"].

Prediction Mechanism

Once the input is tokenized, the model uses its learned patterns to predict the next token in the sequence. For example, given the prompt "The sky is," the model might predict "blue" as the next word based on its training data.

Example:

- **Input Prompt:** "The capital of France is"

- **Model Prediction:** "Paris"

This prediction is based on the model's understanding of the relationship between "France" and "Paris" from its training data.

Generative Capabilities

Modern AI models, such as GPT (Generative Pre-trained Transformer), are generative, meaning they can create entirely new text rather than simply retrieving pre-existing information. This allows them to write essays, generate code, or even compose poetry.

Example:

5. **Input Prompt:** "Write a short poem about the ocean."
6. **Model Output:**

The ocean whispers, deep and wide,
A world of secrets, in its tide.
Waves that dance, in moonlit glow,
A timeless rhythm, ebb and flow.

2.2 Strengths and Limitations of AI Models

AI models are powerful tools, but they are not without their limitations. Understanding both their strengths and weaknesses is essential for using them effectively.

Strengths

7. **Text Generation and Completion**
   AI models excel at generating coherent and contextually relevant text. They can complete sentences, paragraphs, or even entire documents based on a given prompt.
   - **Example:**
     - **Input Prompt:** "The benefits of exercise include"
     - **Model Output:** "improved cardiovascular health, increased muscle strength, better mental health, and enhanced overall well-being."

8. **Following Explicit Instructions**
   When given clear and specific instructions, AI models can perform tasks such as summarizing text, translating languages, or answering questions.
   - **Example:**
     - **Input Prompt:** "Summarize the plot of 'Romeo and Juliet' in one sentence."

- **Model Output:** "Romeo and Juliet is a tragic love story about two young lovers from feuding families whose deaths ultimately reconcile their families."

9. **Pattern Matching and Continuation**

   AI models are adept at recognizing and continuing patterns in text, making them useful for tasks like code completion, story writing, or even generating musical compositions.

   - **Example:**
     - **Input Prompt:** "The Fibonacci sequence starts with 0, 1, 1, 2, 3, 5,"
     - **Model Output:** "8, 13, 21, 34, 55, and so on."

Limitations

4. **Mathematical Precision**

   While AI models can perform basic arithmetic, they are not designed for complex mathematical calculations and may produce incorrect results.

   a. **Example:**
      i. **Input Prompt:** "What is 12345 multiplied by 6789?"
      ii. **Model Output:** "83,882,205" (The correct answer is 83,882,205, but the model may sometimes provide incorrect results for more complex calculations.)

5. **Factual Accuracy Without Hallucination**

   AI models can sometimes "hallucinate" or generate incorrect or fabricated information, especially when asked about obscure or highly specific topics.

   a. **Example:**
      i. **Input Prompt:** "Who invented the telephone in 1876?"
      ii. **Model Output:** "Alexander Graham Bell invented the telephone in 1876." (This is correct, but for less well-known facts, the model might provide inaccurate information.)

6. **Understanding of Current Events Beyond Training Data**

   AI models are trained on data up to a certain point in time and do not have real-time knowledge. They cannot provide information on events or developments that occurred after their training data cutoff.

   a. **Example:**
      i. **Input Prompt:** "What is the latest news on climate change policies in 2023?"

    ii. **Model Output:** "I do not have information on events or developments beyond October 2023." (This response highlights the model's lack of real-time knowledge.)

2.3 Capability Assessment

Before designing complex prompts or relying on AI models for critical tasks, it is essential to assess their capabilities. This involves testing the model with simple tasks and gradually increasing the complexity to understand its strengths and limitations.

Step 1: Start with Simple Tasks

Begin by testing the model with straightforward questions or prompts to gauge its basic functionality.

    5. **Example:**
        a. **Input Prompt:** "What is the capital of Japan?"
        b. **Model Output:** "Tokyo."

Step 2: Increase Complexity

Once the model performs well on simple tasks, introduce more complex prompts to evaluate its ability to handle nuanced or multi-step instructions.

    4. **Example:**
        a. **Input Prompt:** "Explain the process of photosynthesis in simple terms."
        b. **Model Output:** "Photosynthesis is the process by which plants use sunlight, water, and carbon dioxide to create oxygen and energy in the form of sugar."

Step 3: Test for Limitations

Identify the model's limitations by asking questions that require real-time knowledge, complex reasoning, or highly specific expertise.

    4. **Example:**
        a. **Input Prompt:** "What are the latest advancements in quantum computing as of 2023?"
        b. **Model Output:** "I do not have information on events or developments beyond October 2023."

Step 4: Evaluate Consistency

Assess the model's consistency by asking the same question in different ways or requesting multiple iterations of a task.

> 4. **Example:**
>> a. **Input Prompt 1:** "Write a brief summary of the American Revolution."
>> b. **Input Prompt 2:** "Can you provide an overview of the American Revolution?"
>> c. **Model Output:** Both prompts should yield similar summaries, demonstrating the model's consistency.

Step 5: Identify Edge Cases

Test the model with edge cases or ambiguous prompts to understand how it handles uncertainty or incomplete information.

> 4. **Example:**
>> a. **Input Prompt:** "What is the meaning of life?"
>> b. **Model Output:** "The meaning of life is a philosophical question with many interpretations, often related to purpose, existence, and fulfilment."

Step 6: Iterate and Refine

Based on the assessment, refine your prompts and expectations to align with the model's capabilities. This iterative process helps optimize the model's performance for specific tasks.

> 6. **Example:**
>> a. **Initial Prompt:** "Explain quantum mechanics."
>> b. **Refined Prompt:** "Explain the basics of quantum mechanics in simple terms for a high school student."

Practical Applications of Capability Assessment

Understanding how to assess AI models is crucial for their effective application in various fields. Here are some practical examples:

1. Content Creation

AI models can generate blog posts, articles, or marketing copy. However, it's essential to review and edit the output to ensure accuracy and alignment with the intended message.

> 6. **Example:**
>> a. **Input Prompt:** "Write a blog post about the benefits of remote work."

b. **Model Output:** A detailed article discussing flexibility, cost savings, and improved work-life balance.

2. Customer Support

AI models can assist in answering frequently asked questions or providing troubleshooting steps. However, they should be monitored to ensure responses are accurate and helpful.

4. **Example:**
    a. **Input Prompt:** "How do I reset my password?"
    b. **Model Output:** Step-by-step instructions for resetting a password.

3. Education and Tutoring

AI models can explain complex concepts or provide practice problems for students. However, educators should verify the accuracy of the information provided.

7. **Example:**
    o **Input Prompt:** "Explain the Pythagorean theorem."
    o **Model Output:** A clear explanation of the theorem and its application in right-angled triangles.

4. Programming Assistance

AI models can generate code snippets or debug existing code. However, developers should test the code to ensure it functions as intended.

- **Example:**
    o **Input Prompt:** "Write a Python function to calculate the factorial of a number."
    o **Model Output:** A Python function that computes the factorial.

AI models, particularly language models, are powerful tools with a wide range of applications. By understanding how they work, recognizing their strengths and limitations, and systematically assessing their capabilities, users can harness their potential effectively. Whether for content creation, customer support, education, or programming, AI models offer immense value when used thoughtfully and with an awareness of their constraints. As AI technology continues to evolve, so too will our ability to leverage these models for increasingly complex and impactful tasks.

Chapter 3: Core Principles of Prompt Design

PROMPT DESIGN IS A critical aspect of interacting with language models effectively. A well-crafted prompt ensures that the model understands the task, provides relevant and accurate responses, and adheres to any specific requirements. This chapter delves into the core principles of prompt design, focusing on clarity, context, and instruction, and the use of examples and constraints. Each principle is explained in detail, with examples and methods to help you design effective prompts.

3.1 Clarity and Precision

Clarity and precision are the foundation of effective prompt design. A clear and precise prompt ensures that the language model understands exactly what is being asked, reducing the likelihood of irrelevant or incorrect responses. Ambiguity in prompts can lead to confusion, misinterpretation, and outputs that do not meet your expectations.

Why Clarity and Precision Matter

- **Avoids Misinterpretation**: Language models rely on the information provided in the prompt to generate responses. If the prompt is vague, the model may interpret it in unintended ways.
- **Improves Relevance**: Clear prompts help the model focus on the specific task, leading to more relevant and accurate outputs.
- **Saves Time**: Precise prompts reduce the need for follow-up clarifications or corrections.

Methods to Achieve Clarity and Precision

7. **Use Simple and Direct Language**: Avoid overly complex sentences or jargon. For example:
    a. Unclear: "Tell me about the thing that makes people happy."

b. Clear: "Explain the concept of happiness and its psychological benefits."
8. **Specify the Desired Output Format**: If you want a list, paragraph, or bullet points, state it explicitly.
   a. Example: "Provide a list of five benefits of exercise."
9. **Avoid Ambiguous Terms**: Replace vague words with specific ones.
   a. Unclear: "Write something about technology."
   b. Clear: "Write a 200-word summary of the impact of artificial intelligence on healthcare."
10. **Provide Context**: Include background information to guide the model.
   a. Example: "You are a financial advisor. Explain the concept of compound interest to a beginner."
11. **Break Down Complex Tasks**: Divide multi-part questions into smaller, more manageable prompts.
   a. Example: Instead of asking, "Explain the causes and effects of climate change and suggest solutions," break it into:
      i. "What are the main causes of climate change?"
      ii. "What are the effects of climate change on the environment?"
      iii. "What are three potential solutions to mitigate climate change?"

Examples of Clear and Precise Prompts

10. **General Knowledge**: "Explain the process of photosynthesis in plants, including the role of chlorophyll and sunlight."
11. **Creative Writing**: "Write a short story about a robot discovering emotions for the first time. Use a first-person narrative."
12. **Data Analysis**: "Analyse the following dataset and identify the top three trends in sales over the past year."

3.2 Context and Instruction

Providing **context and instruction** is essential for guiding the model's response. Context helps the model understand the background or purpose of the task, while instructions specify how the task should be completed. Without sufficient context and clear instructions, the model may produce generic or off-target responses.

Why Context and Instruction Matter

7. **Guides the Model's Focus**: Context helps the model understand the scope and purpose of the task.
8. **Ensures Consistency**: Clear instructions ensure that the model follows a specific approach or format.
9. **Enhances Creativity**: In creative tasks, context can inspire the model to generate more relevant and imaginative outputs.

Methods to Provide Context and Instruction

6. **Set the Scene**: Describe the scenario or background information.
   a. Example: "You are a historian writing an article about the Industrial Revolution. Explain its impact on urbanization."
7. **Define the Role**: Specify the role the model should assume.
   a. Example: "You are a career counsellor. Provide advice to a recent graduate on choosing a career path."
8. **State the Objective**: Clearly state the goal of the task.
   a. Example: "The goal is to create a persuasive argument for reducing plastic waste."
9. **Use Directives**: Use action-oriented language to guide the model.
   a. Example: "Summarize the key points of the article in three sentences."
10. **Incorporate Constraints**: Specify any limitations or requirements.
    a. Example: "Write a 500-word essay on renewable energy, focusing on solar power."

Examples of Context and Instruction

5. **Educational Context**: "You are a teacher explaining the water cycle to fifth-grade students. Use simple language and include a diagram description."
6. **Business Context**: "You are a marketing consultant. Develop a social media strategy for a new coffee shop targeting young professionals."
7. **Technical Context**: "You are a software engineer. Explain the difference between Python and Java, focusing on syntax and use cases."

3.3 Examples and Constraints

Including **examples and constraints** in your prompts helps the model understand the desired output and adhere to specific requirements. Examples provide a reference for the model to follow, while constraints ensure that the response meets certain criteria.

Why Examples and Constraints Matter

5. **Sets Expectations**: Examples show the model what a good response looks like.
6. **Improves Accuracy**: Constraints narrow down the scope of the response, making it more focused and relevant.
7. **Encourages Creativity**: In creative tasks, constraints can inspire the model to think outside the box while staying within defined boundaries.

Methods to Use Examples and Constraints

5. **Provide Sample Outputs**: Include examples of the desired format or content.
   a. Example: "Write a product description for a smartwatch. Example: 'The XYZ Smartwatch features a heart rate monitor, GPS tracking, and a 7-day battery life.'"
6. **Specify Length or Word Count**: Define how long the response should be.
   a. Example: "Write a 300-word summary of the benefits of meditation."
7. **Set Tone or Style**: Indicate the tone or style of the response.

a. Example: "Write a formal letter to a company requesting a refund for a defective product."
8. **Limit Scope**: Define the boundaries of the response.
   a. Example: "Discuss the benefits of electric cars but avoid discussing environmental concerns."
9. **Incorporate Formatting Requirements**: Specify any formatting needs.
   a. Example: "Create a bullet-point list of the top five features of a smartphone."

Examples of Prompts with Examples and Constraints

5. **Creative Writing**: "Write a poem about the ocean. Example: 'The waves whisper secrets to the shore, a timeless dance forevermore.' Constraint: Use rhyming couplets."
6. **Technical Writing**: "Explain the concept of blockchain technology. Example: 'Blockchain is a decentralized ledger that records transactions across multiple computers.' Constraint: Use no more than 200 words."
7. **Business Writing**: "Draft an email to a client introducing a new service. Example: 'Dear [Client], we are excited to introduce our new consulting service designed to help businesses streamline operations.' Constraint: Keep the email under 150 words."

Combining Principles for Effective Prompt Design

To create highly effective prompts, combine the principles of clarity and precision, context and instruction, and examples and constraints. Here's how you can integrate these principles:

7. **Start with Clarity**: Ensure your prompt is clear and precise.
8. **Add Context and Instructions**: Provide background information and specific directions.
9. **Include Examples and Constraints**: Offer examples and define any limitations.

Example of a Combined Prompt

7. **Task**: Write a blog post about the benefits of remote work.

8. **Clarity and Precision**: "Write a 500-word blog post about the benefits of remote work for employees and employers."
9. **Context and Instruction**: "You are a career coach writing for an audience of professionals. Focus on productivity, work-life balance, and cost savings."
10. **Examples and Constraints**: "Example: 'Remote work allows employees to save time on commuting, leading to increased productivity.' Constraint: Include at least three statistics to support your points."

Common Pitfalls to Avoid

5. **Overloading the Prompt**: Avoid including too much information, which can confuse the model.
6. **Being Too Vague**: Lack of specificity can lead to irrelevant responses.
7. **Ignoring Constraints**: Failing to define constraints may result in outputs that don't meet your needs.
8. **Neglecting Context**: Without context, the model may produce generic or off-topic responses.

Mastering the core principles of prompt design clarity and precision, context and instruction, and examples and constraints enables you to interact with language models more effectively. By applying these principles, you can craft prompts that yield accurate, relevant, and high-quality responses. Whether you're seeking information, generating creative content, or solving complex problems, thoughtful prompt design is the key to unlocking the full potential of language models.

Chapter 4: Structured Prompting

HARNESSING PRECISION and clarity to optimize AI interactions.

4.1 Anatomy of a Prompt

A well-structured prompt is a blueprint for effective AI communication. Breaking it into core components ensures clarity and direction. Below are the six elements, each with examples:

1. **Instruction**
   What to Do: Direct commands guide the AI.
   - *Example*: "Translate the following English paragraph to French."
   - *Method*: Use imperative verbs (e.g., "Summarize," "Analyse").

2. **Context**
   Background Information: Sets the scene or role.
   - *Example*: "You are a nutritionist advising a diabetic patient. Explain the benefits of a low-carb diet."
   - *Method*: Define roles, scenarios, or objectives explicitly.

3. **Input Data**
   Provided Information: The raw material for the AI to process.
   - *Example*: "Text: [Insert customer feedback here]."
   - *Method*: Use placeholders (e.g., [text], [data]) for dynamic inputs.

4. **Output Format**
   Structure Requirements: Specifies how results should appear.
   - *Example*: "Present results as a markdown table with columns 'Metric' and 'Value'."
   - *Method*: Define formats (e.g., JSON, bullet points, paragraphs).

5. **Examples**
   Input-Output Pairs: Illustrate desired outcomes.
   - *Example*:
     - *Input*: "Review: The battery life is excellent."

- *Output*: "Sentiment: Positive. Feature: Battery."
  - o *Method*: Include 1–2 examples to reduce ambiguity.

6. **Constraints**

Limitations: Boundaries for content or style.
  - o *Example*: "Use layman's terms and avoid technical jargon."
  - o *Method*: List restrictions (e.g., word count, tone, excluded topics).

4.2 Using Templates

Templates standardize prompts for repeatable tasks, enhancing efficiency and consistency. Below are three use cases with methods:

12. **Customer Service Template**
    a. *Structure*:

Role: Support agent specializing in [industry].
Task: Respond to a customer complaint about [issue].
Tone: [Empathetic/Professional].
Output: [Email/Chat response] with [key points].

13. *Example*: Resolving a refund request for an e-commerce platform.

10. **Creative Writing Template**
    a. *Structure*:

Genre: [Fantasy/Sci-Fi].
Characters: [Protagonist + Antagonist].
Plot Elements: [Conflict + Resolution].
Style: [Descriptive/Concise].

11. *Example*: Generating a fantasy short story with a hero's journey arc.

8. **Data Analysis Template**
    a. *Structure*:

Dataset: [Describe data type, e.g., sales figures].
Task: Identify trends in [time period].
Output: [Graph + Summary] highlighting top 3 insights.

8. *Example*: Analyzing quarterly revenue data for a retail chain.

Benefits of Templates:

10. **Consistency**: Uniform outputs across teams.
11. **Scalability**: Easily adapt to similar tasks.
12. **Error Reduction**: Prevents omissions of critical details.

4.3 Best Practices for Structured Prompts
Refine prompts using these strategies, illustrated with examples:

8. **Use Clear Sections with Headers**
   a. *Good Example*:### Instruction ###

Summarize the text below.
Context
Audience: Middle school students.
Output Format
3 bullet points, each under 15 words.

10. *Poor Example*: A wall of text without headers.
11. *Method*: Label sections (e.g., ## Instruction ##) for readability.

11. **Minimize Ambiguity**
   a. *Vague*: "Write about climate change."
   b. *Specific*: "Write a 300-word blog post explaining climate change's impact on polar bears for a teen audience."
   c. *Method*: Use quantifiable metrics (e.g., word count, audience).
12. **Balance Conciseness and Completeness**
   a. *Too Wordy*: "In a detailed manner, considering all possible factors, describe..."
   b. *Balanced*: "Explain three economic factors influencing inflation in 200 words."
   c. *Method*: Trim redundant phrases while retaining critical details.

Advanced Techniques:

9. **Iterative Testing**: Refine prompts based on AI outputs.
10.   **A/B Testing**: Compare two prompt versions for effectiveness.
11.   **Tool Integration**: Use platforms like OpenAI Playground to validate structures.

Case Study: Improving Tech Support Responses
Before: Unstructured prompts led to inconsistent replies.
After: Implementing a template with role, task, and tone reduced resolution time by 40%.
Pitfalls to Avoid:

8. Overloading prompts with unnecessary constraints.
9. Assuming the AI infers unstated context.

Structured prompting transforms vague queries into precise tools for AI collaboration. By dissecting prompts into components, standardizing with templates, and adhering to best practices, users unlock consistent, high-quality outputs. Whether for business, education, or creativity, mastering this skill ensures efficient and reliable AI interactions.

Chapter 5: Chain of Thought and Reasoning

BREAKING DOWN COMPLEX problems into smaller, manageable steps is a fundamental strategy for guiding models through the reasoning process. This approach not only simplifies the task for the model but also enhances its ability to generate accurate and coherent responses. Here's how you can effectively break down complex problems:

1. Identify the Core Problem

- Start by clearly defining the main problem or question. This helps in understanding what needs to be solved and sets the direction for the subsequent steps.
- **Example:** If the problem is to "Explain the impact of climate change on agriculture," the core problem is understanding the relationship between climate change and agricultural productivity.

2. List Sub-Problems

13.   Divide the core problem into smaller, more specific sub-problems. Each sub-problem should address a particular aspect of the main issue.

14.   **Example:** Sub-problems for the climate change impact on agriculture could include:
   a. How does temperature rise affect crop yields?
   b. What is the impact of changing precipitation patterns on farming?
   c. How do extreme weather events influence agricultural practices?

3. Prioritize Sub-Problems

14.   Determine the order in which the sub-problems should be addressed. Some sub-problems may be

prerequisites for others, or some may be more critical to the overall solution.

15.   **Example:** Understanding temperature rise might be prioritized over extreme weather events because it is a more fundamental aspect of climate change.

4. Develop Solutions for Each Sub-Problem

11.   Address each sub-problem individually, ensuring that the solutions are clear and well-reasoned. This step-by-step approach helps in building a comprehensive solution to the main problem.

12.   **Example:** For the sub-problem "How does temperature rise affect crop yields?" you might explain the physiological effects of higher temperatures on plants, such as increased water stress or altered growth cycles.

5. Integrate Solutions

12.   Combine the solutions to the sub-problems to form a cohesive answer to the main problem. Ensure that the integration is logical and that the solutions complement each other.

13.   **Example:** After addressing temperature rise, changing precipitation patterns, and extreme weather events, you can integrate these findings to provide a holistic view of how climate change impacts agriculture.

6. Validate the Solution

9. Review the integrated solution to ensure it adequately addresses the main problem. Check for consistency, completeness, and accuracy.

10.   **Example:** Verify that the explanation of climate change's impact on agriculture covers all major aspects and that the reasoning is sound.

7. Refine and Simplify

9. Refine the solution to make it more concise and easier to understand. Remove any unnecessary details or redundancies.

10. **Example:** Simplify the explanation by focusing on the most significant impacts of climate change on agriculture, such as reduced crop yields and increased vulnerability to pests.

8. Use Analogies and Examples

13. Analogies and examples can help in making complex problems more relatable and easier to understand. They provide a concrete reference point for abstract concepts.

14. **Example:** To explain the impact of temperature rise on crops, you might use the analogy of a plant being like a machine that operates optimally within a certain temperature range. If the temperature exceeds this range, the machine (plant) becomes less efficient.

9. Visual Aids

9. Visual aids such as diagrams, charts, and graphs can be incredibly helpful in breaking down complex problems. They provide a visual representation of the relationships between different components of the problem.

10. **Example:** A graph showing the correlation between rising temperatures and declining crop yields can make the relationship more tangible.

10. Iterative Approach

12. Complex problems often require an iterative approach, where you repeatedly refine and adjust your understanding and solutions as you gather more information.

13. **Example:** If new research emerges showing that certain crops are more resilient to temperature changes than previously thought, you would need to adjust your explanation accordingly.

11. Collaborative Problem Solving

13.   Sometimes, breaking down complex problems is more effective when done collaboratively. Different perspectives can help in identifying sub-problems and solutions that you might not have considered on your own.

14.   **Example:** Working with a team of experts in climate science and agriculture can provide a more comprehensive understanding of the problem.

12. Use of Frameworks

12.   Frameworks such as SWOT analysis (Strengths, Weaknesses, Opportunities, Threats) or the 5 Whys can be useful in systematically breaking down complex problems.

13.   **Example:** Applying the 5 Whys to the problem of declining crop yields might reveal underlying issues such as soil degradation or inadequate irrigation.

13. Scenario Analysis

10.   Scenario analysis involves exploring different possible outcomes based on varying assumptions. This can help in understanding the range of potential impacts of a complex problem.

11.   **Example:** Analyzing different scenarios of climate change (e.g., moderate vs. severe temperature rise) can help in understanding the varying impacts on agriculture.

14. Feedback Loops

- Incorporating feedback loops allows you to continuously refine your understanding of the problem and the effectiveness of your solutions.
- **Example:** After implementing a new agricultural practice to mitigate the impact of climate change, you would monitor its effectiveness and make adjustments as needed.

15. Documentation

- Documenting each step of the problem-solving process ensures that you have a clear record of your reasoning and can easily revisit and refine your approach if needed.
- **Example:** Keeping a detailed record of how you broke down the problem of climate change's impact on agriculture, including the sub-problems identified and the solutions developed, can be invaluable for future reference.

5.2 Implementing Chain of Thought

Chain of Thought (CoT) reasoning is a technique that involves guiding the model through a series of logical steps to arrive at a solution. This approach is particularly useful for complex problems that require multi-step reasoning. Here are some methods to implement CoT:

1. Zero-Shot CoT

- In Zero-Shot CoT, the model is prompted to generate a step-by-step reasoning process without any prior examples. This method relies on the model's ability to infer the necessary steps based on the prompt.
- **Example:** Prompt: "Explain how photosynthesis works." The model might generate a response that breaks down the process into steps such as light absorption, water splitting, and carbon fixation.

2. Few-Shot CoT

- Few-Shot CoT involves providing the model with a few examples of step-by-step reasoning before asking it to solve a new problem. This helps the model understand the expected format and depth of reasoning.
- **Example:** Before asking the model to explain how a car engine works, you might provide examples of how to explain other mechanical processes, such as how a bicycle works.

3. Explicit Step-by-Step Instructions

- Providing explicit instructions for each step of the reasoning process can help guide the model more effectively. This method ensures that the model follows a logical sequence.
- **Example:** Prompt: "Step 1: Identify the main components of a computer. Step 2: Explain the function of each component. Step 3: Describe how the components work together."

4. Use of Intermediate Questions

- Asking intermediate questions can help the model break down the problem into smaller parts and address each part sequentially.
- **Example:** Instead of asking "How does a computer work?" you might ask "What are the main components of a computer?" followed by "What is the function of the CPU?"

5. Visualization of Thought Process

- Encouraging the model to visualize its thought process can help in making the reasoning more transparent and easier to follow.
- **Example:** Prompt: "Imagine you are explaining how a computer works to a child. Draw a simple diagram in your mind and describe each part as you go."

6. Analogies and Metaphors

- Using analogies and metaphors can help the model relate complex concepts to more familiar ones, making the reasoning process more intuitive.
- **Example:** "Think of a computer as a kitchen. The CPU is like the chef, the RAM is like the countertop, and the hard drive is like the pantry."

7. Iterative Refinement

- Iterative refinement involves repeatedly refining the model's reasoning process by providing feedback and asking for clarifications.

- **Example:** After the model provides an initial explanation, you might ask "Can you elaborate on how the CPU processes instructions?" to encourage deeper reasoning.

8. Use of Hypothetical Scenarios

- Hypothetical scenarios can help the model explore different aspects of a problem and consider various outcomes.
- **Example:** "What would happen if a computer had no RAM? How would that affect its performance?"

9. Breaking Down into Sub-Tasks

- Breaking down the problem into sub-tasks and addressing each one separately can help the model manage complexity more effectively.
- **Example:** Instead of asking "How does a computer process data?" you might break it down into "How does the CPU fetch instructions?" and "How does the CPU execute instructions?"

10. Use of External Knowledge

- Incorporating external knowledge, such as scientific principles or historical context, can enrich the model's reasoning process.
- **Example:** When explaining how a computer works, you might reference the history of computing and how early computers were designed.

11. Encouraging Self-Questioning

- Encouraging the model to ask itself questions can help it explore different angles of the problem and deepen its understanding.
- **Example:** "What are the key components of a computer? How do they interact with each other? What are the potential bottlenecks in the system?"

12. Use of Structured Formats

- Using structured formats such as bullet points or numbered lists can help the model organize its thoughts more clearly.
- **Example:** Prompt: "List the steps involved in booting up a computer: 1. Power on, 2. BIOS initialization, 3. Operating system load, etc."

13. Incorporating Counterfactuals

- Exploring counterfactual scenarios can help the model consider alternative explanations and solutions.
- **Example:** "What if computers were designed without a CPU? How would that change the way they process information?"

14. Use of Mnemonics

- Mnemonics can help the model remember complex sequences or concepts by associating them with simpler, more memorable phrases.
- **Example:** To remember the steps in the scientific method, the model might use the mnemonic "Please Help Einstein Make A New Theory" (Problem, Hypothesis, Experiment, Analysis, Conclusion).

15. Encouraging Reflection

- Encouraging the model to reflect on its reasoning process can help it identify gaps or errors and improve its understanding.
- **Example:** After providing an explanation, you might ask "Does this explanation cover all the key points? Is there anything you might have missed?"

5.3 Examples of Multi-Step Reasoning

Multi-step reasoning involves guiding the model through a series of logical steps to arrive at a solution. Here are some examples that demonstrate how to guide the model through multi-step reasoning tasks:

1. Mathematical Problem Solving

- **Problem:** "If a train travels 300 miles in 5 hours, what is its average speed?"
- **Step 1:** Identify the formula for average speed: Speed = Distance / Time.
- **Step 2:** Plug in the values: Speed = 300 miles / 5 hours.
- **Step 3:** Calculate the result: Speed = 60 miles per hour.

2. Scientific Explanation

- **Problem:** "Explain the process of photosynthesis."
- **Step 1:** Describe the role of sunlight in photosynthesis: Sunlight provides the energy needed to drive the process.
- **Step 2:** Explain the absorption of light by chlorophyll: Chlorophyll in plant cells absorbs light, primarily in the blue and red wavelengths.
- **Step 3:** Describe the splitting of water molecules: The energy from light is used to split water molecules into oxygen and hydrogen.
- **Step 4:** Explain the fixation of carbon dioxide: The hydrogen from water is used to convert carbon dioxide into glucose.

3. Historical Analysis

- **Problem:** "What were the causes of World War I?"
- **Step 1:** Identify the main causes: Militarism, Alliances, Imperialism, and Nationalism.
- **Step 2:** Explain militarism: The arms race among European powers increased tensions.
- **Step 3:** Discuss alliances: The complex web of alliances meant that a conflict between two countries could quickly escalate.
- **Step 4:** Describe imperialism: Competition for colonies created rivalries among European nations.
- **Step 5:** Explain nationalism: Intense national pride and desire for independence fueled conflicts.

4. Literary Analysis

- **Problem:** "Analyze the theme of love in Shakespeare's 'Romeo and Juliet.'"
- **Step 1:** Identify the different types of love in the play: Romantic love, familial love, and friendship.
- **Step 2:** Discuss romantic love: The passionate love between Romeo and Juliet is the central theme.
- **Step 3:** Explore familial love: The love between Juliet and her family, particularly her parents, is strained by the feud.
- **Step 4:** Examine friendship: The loyalty between Romeo and his friends, such as Mercutio, plays a significant role in the plot.

5. Economic Analysis

- **Problem:** "Explain the impact of inflation on the economy."
- **Step 1:** Define inflation: Inflation is the rate at which the general level of prices for goods and services is rising.
- **Step 2:** Discuss the causes of inflation: Demand-pull inflation, cost-push inflation, and built-in inflation.
- **Step 3:** Explain the effects on consumers: Inflation reduces the purchasing power of money, making goods and services more expensive.
- **Step 4:** Describe the impact on businesses: Inflation can increase the cost of production, leading to higher prices for consumers.
- **Step 5:** Discuss the role of government: Central banks may raise interest rates to control inflation, which can slow economic growth.

6. Technical Troubleshooting

- **Problem:** "My computer won't turn on. What should I do?"
- **Step 1:** Check the power source: Ensure the computer is plugged in and the power outlet is working.
- **Step 2:** Inspect the power cable: Look for any visible damage to the cable.
- **Step 3:** Test the power button: Press the power button to see if there is any response.

- **Step 4:** Check the internal components: If the computer still won't turn on, open the case and check for loose connections or damaged components.
- **Step 5:** Seek professional help: If the issue persists, consult a technician for further diagnosis.

7. Legal Reasoning

- **Problem:** "Is it legal to download music from the internet?"
- **Step 1:** Define copyright law: Copyright law protects the rights of creators to control the use of their work.
- **Step 2:** Discuss the legality of downloading music: Downloading music without permission from the copyright holder is generally illegal.
- **Step 3:** Explore exceptions: Some music may be available for free download under a Creative Commons license.
- **Step 4:** Consider the consequences: Illegal downloading can result in fines or legal action.
- **Step 5:** Recommend legal alternatives: Suggest using legal streaming services or purchasing music from authorized sellers.

8. Medical Diagnosis

- **Problem:** "A patient presents with a fever, cough, and shortness of breath. What could be the cause?"
- **Step 1:** List possible causes: Common cold, flu, pneumonia, COVID-19.
- **Step 2:** Evaluate symptoms: Fever and cough are common in all, but shortness of breath is more indicative of pneumonia or COVID-19.
- **Step 3:** Consider patient history: Recent travel or exposure to sick individuals could suggest COVID-19.
- **Step 4:** Recommend diagnostic tests: A chest X-ray or COVID-19 test may be necessary.
- **Step 5:** Suggest treatment: Depending on the diagnosis, treatment may include rest, fluids, or antiviral medication.

9. Environmental Impact Assessment

- **Problem:** "What are the environmental impacts of deforestation?"
- **Step 1:** Define deforestation: The large-scale removal of trees from forests.
- **Step 2:** Discuss loss of biodiversity: Deforestation leads to habitat destruction, threatening many species.
- **Step 3:** Explain climate change: Trees absorb carbon dioxide; their removal contributes to increased greenhouse gases.
- **Step 4:** Describe soil erosion: Without trees, soil is more susceptible to erosion, leading to loss of fertile land.
- **Step 5:** Suggest solutions: Reforestation, sustainable logging practices, and conservation efforts can mitigate the impacts.

10. Psychological Analysis

- **Problem:** "What are the effects of stress on mental health?"
- **Step 1:** Define stress: A physiological response to perceived threats or challenges.
- **Step 2:** Discuss short-term effects: Stress can cause anxiety, irritability, and difficulty concentrating.
- **Step 3:** Explore long-term effects: Chronic stress can lead to depression, burnout, and other mental health disorders.
- **Step 4:** Explain the physiological impact: Stress triggers the release of cortisol, which can affect brain function.
- **Step 5:** Suggest coping mechanisms: Techniques such as mindfulness, exercise, and therapy can help manage stress.

11. Business Strategy Development

- **Problem:** "How can a small business increase its market share?"
- **Step 1:** Analyse the current market: Identify competitors, customer needs, and market trends.
- **Step 2:** Develop a unique value proposition: Offer something that competitors do not, such as superior customer service or a unique product feature.
- **Step 3:** Implement marketing strategies: Use social media, content marketing, and SEO to reach a wider audience.

- **Step 4:** Focus on customer retention: Provide excellent customer service and loyalty programs to keep existing customers.
- **Step 5:** Monitor and adjust: Continuously track performance and adjust strategies as needed.

12. Ethical Dilemma Resolution

- **Problem:** "Is it ethical to use animals for scientific research?"
- **Step 1:** Define ethical considerations: The moral principles that guide decision-making.
- **Step 2:** Discuss the benefits: Animal research has led to medical breakthroughs that save human lives.
- **Step 3:** Explore the ethical concerns: The suffering and death of animals raise moral questions.
- **Step 4:** Consider alternatives: In vitro testing, computer modelling, and human volunteers are potential alternatives.
- **Step 5:** Weigh the pros and cons: Balance the potential benefits against the ethical concerns to make an informed decision.

Chapter 6: Prompt Chaining and Task Decomposition

PROMPT ENGINEERING is evolving from a simple one-shot interaction to complex, multi-step workflows where each prompt builds on the output of a previous one. In this chapter, we explore how to chain prompts together and decompose large tasks into manageable subtasks that not only improve accuracy but also provide structured, high-quality outputs. We will discuss methods for breaking down tasks, managing data flow between prompts, and implementing robust error handling and recovery mechanisms. Throughout, we include a variety of examples, explanations, and methods 15 distinct approaches to illustrate best practices and creative techniques for advanced prompt chaining and task decomposition.

6.1 Breaking Tasks into Subtasks

Large, multifaceted tasks can overwhelm even the most sophisticated language models. To overcome these limitations, it is essential to decompose a complex task into smaller, more focused subtasks. By breaking down a larger problem, you allow the model to address one aspect at a time, thereby improving precision and clarity.

Method 1: Hierarchical Decomposition

Explanation:

Hierarchical decomposition involves creating a task hierarchy, where the main task is broken into primary subtasks, which are then further divided if necessary.

Example:

Imagine you need to generate a comprehensive market analysis report. The main task can be decomposed into:

Subtask A: Research market trends.

Subtask B: Analyse competitor performance.

Subtask C: Forecast future market growth.

Each of these subtasks can be further refined. For instance, "Research market trends" might be broken down into gathering historical data, analyzing recent shifts, and synthesizing expert opinions.

Method 2: Sequential Step-by-Step Decomposition

Explanation:

This method works by arranging subtasks in a logical sequence where each step's output becomes the input for the next step.

Example:

For writing a technical manual:

Step 1: Draft an outline of sections.

Step 2: For each section, list key topics.

Step 3: Write detailed explanations for each topic.

Step 4: Combine and edit for consistency.

This approach ensures that the final output is built incrementally and thoroughly.

Method 3: Parallel Decomposition

Explanation:

When tasks are independent, they can be processed in parallel, and the results are later aggregated.

Example:

For an e-commerce website, if you need to generate product descriptions for multiple categories, each category can be handled independently:

Subtask A: Generate descriptions for electronics.

Subtask B: Generate descriptions for apparel.

Subtask C: Generate descriptions for home appliances.

After processing in parallel, a final prompt can be used to standardize the tone and style across all categories.

Method 4: Role-Based Decomposition

Explanation:

Assigning specific roles to different subtasks can optimize outputs by tailoring instructions according to the required expertise.

Example:

For a legal document analysis, assign:

Role 1: Contract Analysis Expert to review clauses.

Role 2: Regulatory Specialist to evaluate compliance.

Role 3: Risk Analyst to identify potential issues.

Each role focuses on a distinct component of the overall task, and their outputs are integrated to form a complete analysis.

6.2 Managing Data Flow Between Prompts

Efficient prompt chaining depends on the seamless transfer of data between prompts. Establishing explicit schemas and formats for input and output ensures that essential information is preserved and transformed accurately throughout the process.

Method 5: Defining Explicit Data Schemas

Explanation:

Create a structured schema to standardize the data format exchanged between prompts.

Example:

Suppose the output of Prompt 1 is a list of key market trends. Define a JSON schema such as:

In json

```
{
"trends": [
{"name": "Trend A", "impact": "High", "description": "Details about Trend A"},
{"name": "Trend B", "impact": "Medium", "description": "Details about Trend B"}
]
}
```

Subsequent prompts can then reference this structured data to generate a coherent market analysis.

Method 6: Using Inter-Prompt Variables

Explanation:

Store specific pieces of information as variables to be reused in subsequent prompts.

Example:

When analyzing a customer review process, assign key metrics (like satisfaction scores or recurring issues) to variables such as {{satisfaction_score}} and {{issue_summary}}. The next prompt can incorporate these variables to create a summary report without re-extracting the data.

Method 7: Data Compression and Summarization

Explanation:

For lengthy outputs, use summarization techniques to compress the data before passing it to the next prompt.

Example:

If a detailed research paper is processed in multiple steps, have an intermediate prompt that produces a concise summary (e.g., 100–

200 words) which captures the key points. This summary is then used as the context for further analysis or rewriting.

Method 8: Utilizing Templates for Consistent Data Flow

Explanation:

Templates standardize the format of inputs and outputs, reducing ambiguity and ensuring consistency across prompt chains.

Example:

Design a template for a product review analysis:

In css

```
[TASK]: Analyze product reviews.
[INPUT]:
{
"reviews": [
{"id": 1, "text": "Review text here", "rating": 4},
{"id": 2, "text": "Another review text", "rating": 5}
]
}
[OUTPUT FORMAT]:
{
"overall_sentiment": "Positive/Negative/Neutral",
"key_issues": ["issue1", "issue2"],
"recommendations": "Improvement suggestions"
}
```

This template ensures that all outputs follow a predetermined structure, which can then be reliably parsed by the next prompt.

6.3 Error Handling and Recovery

Errors and inconsistencies are inevitable in complex prompt chains. Effective error handling and recovery protocols are crucial to ensure that the overall system remains robust and that minor issues do not derail the entire workflow.

Method 9: Built-In Validation Checks

Explanation:

Incorporate validation checks at each stage of the prompt chain to verify that outputs meet defined criteria before they are passed on.

Example:

If a prompt outputs a JSON object, include a subsequent validation prompt that checks for required keys (e.g., "trends", "ratings"). If keys are missing, the system can either request a re-run of the previous step or flag an error.

46

Method 10: Fallback Prompts
Explanation:
Design fallback prompts that automatically trigger when an error is detected.
Example:
For a task that involves generating statistical analysis, if the output does not include necessary figures, a fallback prompt can instruct:
"Re-run the analysis using the provided dataset and ensure that statistical measures (mean, median, mode) are included in your response."
Method 11: Iterative Refinement with Feedback Loops
Explanation:
Implement a system where outputs are iteratively refined based on error feedback.
Example:
For a multi-step customer service scenario, if the initial response lacks clarity, a feedback prompt can request:
"Review the previous answer and add more details about the resolution process. Please rephrase for clarity."
This iterative approach helps to fine-tune the output until it meets quality standards.
Method 12: Error Logging and Monitoring
Explanation:
Maintain a log of errors and the conditions under which they occur to help improve the prompt design over time.
Example:
For an enterprise-level prompt chain, errors such as "missing data" or "format inconsistencies" are recorded with timestamp, input data, and error type. Periodic reviews of these logs allow prompt engineers to identify recurring issues and update templates or protocols accordingly.
6.4 Using Templates to Standardize Prompts
Templates are powerful tools that ensure consistency and efficiency in prompt design. They provide a reusable framework that guides the structure and formatting of prompts across various tasks.
Method 13: Standard Template Creation
Explanation:

Develop standard templates that encapsulate common prompt elements such as instructions, context, input data, desired output format, and constraints.

Example:

A template for a market analysis task might be:

[TASK]: Conduct a market analysis for [industry].

[CONTEXT]: Provide an overview of current trends, key players, and potential growth opportunities.

[INPUT]: { "data": "raw market data here" }

[OUTPUT FORMAT]: { "summary": "", "key_trends": [], "recommendations": "" }

[CONSTRAINTS]: Response must be under 500 words and include at least three actionable insights.

By reusing this template across different industries, you ensure a uniform approach that can be easily adapted.

Method 14: Dynamic Template Customization

Explanation:

Allow for dynamic modification of templates based on task-specific parameters.

Example:

When generating content for different types of reports (e.g., financial vs. technical), adjust the template headers, sections, and required data fields. A financial report template might include sections for "Revenue Analysis" and "Expense Breakdown," whereas a technical report might focus on "Feature Analysis" and "Performance Metrics." This adaptability improves relevance without sacrificing consistency.

6.5 Best Practices for Structured Prompts

To get the best results from your prompt chains, it's essential to follow best practices for structured prompting. These guidelines help maintain clarity, reduce ambiguity, and ensure that outputs are both concise and comprehensive.

Method 15: Clear Sectioning with Headers

Explanation:

Organize prompts into clearly defined sections using headers and bullet points. This structure guides the model and makes it easier to follow.

Example:

For a multi-part analysis prompt, structure your prompt as follows:

[INSTRUCTION]: Analyze the following customer feedback.
[SECTION 1: Overview]
- Provide a summary of the overall sentiment.
[SECTION 2: Key Issues]
- List the most frequently mentioned problems.
[SECTION 3: Recommendations]
- Suggest actionable improvements.

This clear breakdown helps the model understand the expectations for each part of the output.

Best Practices Summary:

Clarity and Specificity: Use unambiguous language and clear instructions.

Balanced Detail: Provide enough context to guide the model but avoid overloading it with unnecessary information.

Consistency: Use templates and standardized formats to ensure uniformity across outputs.

Error Resilience: Build in validation, fallback, and iterative feedback mechanisms to handle errors gracefully.

Customization: Adapt templates dynamically to suit the needs of various tasks while maintaining a consistent core structure.

Practical Examples and Applications

Throughout this chapter, we have discussed numerous methods and examples. Here is a summary list of the 15 distinct types of examples/explanations and methods covered:

Hierarchical Decomposition: Breaking a market analysis into research, competitor analysis, and forecasting.

Sequential Step-by-Step Decomposition: Outlining steps to write a technical manual.

Parallel Decomposition: Generating product descriptions for different categories simultaneously.

Role-Based Decomposition: Assigning specialized roles for legal document analysis.

Explicit Data Schemas: Defining a JSON schema for transferring market trends.

Inter-Prompt Variables: Using stored variables like {{satisfaction_score}} in subsequent prompts.

Data Compression and Summarization: Summarizing a research paper for further analysis.

Using Templates: Standardizing outputs using a structured template for product review analysis.

Built-In Validation Checks: Verifying JSON output keys before passing data to the next prompt.

Fallback Prompts: Triggering a re-run if required data is missing.

Iterative Refinement with Feedback Loops: Requesting rephrasing for clarity in customer service responses.

Error Logging and Monitoring: Recording and analyzing errors for continuous improvement.

Standard Template Creation: Developing a market analysis template with defined sections.

Dynamic Template Customization: Adjusting templates based on the task type (financial vs. technical reports).

Clear Sectioning with Headers: Structuring prompts with headers and bullet points to guide output.

Effective prompt chaining and task decomposition are foundational skills in advanced prompt engineering. By breaking complex tasks into manageable subtasks, managing the flow of data between prompts using explicit schemas and templates, and implementing robust error handling and recovery methods, you can significantly enhance the performance of AI models. These techniques not only lead to more accurate and reliable outputs but also pave the way for scalable, enterprise-level AI solutions.

In this chapter, we explored distinct methods and examples from hierarchical and sequential decomposition to dynamic template customization and clear sectioning each designed to help you master the art and science of prompt chaining. As you apply these techniques, remember that iterative refinement and constant feedback are key to optimizing your prompt chains. The ability to structure, validate, and adapt your prompts will empower you to harness the full potential of AI, making your workflows more efficient, resilient, and aligned with your goals.

As the field of AI continues to evolve, so too will the methods of prompt engineering. The strategies outlined here serve as a roadmap for navigating current challenges and anticipating future developments. With these tools in hand, you are well-equipped to design advanced prompt chains that not only meet the demands of complex tasks but also drive innovation across various domains.

Embrace the power of prompt chaining and task decomposition to transform the way you interact with AI. By systematically breaking down tasks, managing data flow effectively, and planning for errors before they occur, you lay the groundwork for a more intelligent, responsive, and adaptable AI-driven future.

Chapter 7: Advanced Prompting Techniques

ADVANCED PROMPTING techniques refine how models approach complexity, robustness, and creativity. Below are 15 methods, explanations, and examples for each of the three core strategies: **Recursive Decomposition**, **Adversarial Thinking**, and **Analogical Reasoning**.

7.1 Recursive Decomposition

Break complex problems into simpler sub-problems, solve each independently, then combine results.

1. **Divide-and-Conquer Algorithms**
   - *Method*: Split a problem into smaller parts, solve each part, and merge solutions (e.g., merge sort).
   - *Example*: Ask the model to summarize a long article by first summarizing individual paragraphs, then combining them.
2. **Stepwise Refinement**
   - *Method*: Iteratively add detail to a high-level solution until fully resolved.
   - *Example*: Prompt: "Plan a novel: Start with a three-act structure, then flesh out scenes, dialogue, and character arcs."
3. **Hierarchical Structuring**
   - *Method*: Organize problems into parent-child relationships (e.g., outlines).
   - *Example*: "Explain quantum computing: Begin with core principles (superposition, entanglement), then dive into hardware and algorithms."
4. **Modular Design**
   - *Method*: Treat components as interchangeable modules.

- *Example*: "Design a recipe app: Separate modules for user profiles, recipe databases, and search functionality."
5. **Dependency Graphs**
   - *Method*: Map sub-problem dependencies to resolve them in order.
   - *Example*: "Debug a program: Identify which functions depend on others to trace error origins."
6. **Parallel Processing**
   - *Method*: Solve independent sub-problems simultaneously.
   - *Example*: "Analyse a dataset: Split data into chunks, compute statistics for each, then aggregate results."
7. **Mathematical Induction**
   - *Method*: Prove a base case, then assume n to solve $n+1$.
   - *Example*: "Calculate Fibonacci sequence: Solve for small numbers first, then generalize the pattern."
8. **Functional Decomposition**
   - *Method*: Break systems into functional units (e.g., input, process, output).
   - *Example*: "Explain photosynthesis: Split into light absorption, Calvin cycle, and glucose synthesis."
9. **Layered Architectures**
   - *Method*: Solve problems layer-by-layer (e.g., OSI model in networking).
   - *Example*: "Describe internet communication: Start with physical cables, then protocols like TCP/IP, then application layers."
10. **Iterative Breakdown**
    - *Method*: Repeatedly split problems until they're trivial.
    - *Example*: "Write a thesis: Divide into chapters, sections, and paragraphs, refining each iteratively."
11. **Problem Trees**
    - *Method*: Visualize root causes and effects as branches.

- *Example*: "Address poverty: Identify roots (education gaps, unemployment), then map solutions to each branch."

12. **System Decomposition**
    - *Method*: Split complex systems into subsystems (e.g., engine parts in a car).
    - *Example*: "Explain climate change: Break into atmospheric science, human activity, and ecosystem impacts."

13. **Object-Oriented Design**
    - *Method*: Model problems as objects with properties and interactions.
    - *Example*: "Simulate a city: Define objects like 'traffic light' and 'pedestrian' with rules for interaction."

14. **Workflow Segmentation**
    - *Method*: Divide processes into sequential stages.
    - *Example*: "Optimize supply chains: Split into procurement, production, distribution, and retail stages."

15. **Recursive Algorithms**
    - *Method*: Solve problems by referencing smaller instances of themselves.
    - *Example*: "Traverse a directory: List files in a folder, then repeat for each subfolder."

7.2 Adversarial Thinking

Propose solutions and actively seek flaws to improve robustness.

15. **Red Teaming**
    a. *Method*: Role-play as an attacker to find weaknesses.
    b. *Example*: "Critique this cybersecurity protocol: How would a hacker bypass two-factor authentication?"

16. **Counterfactual Analysis**
    a. *Method*: Ask "What if?" to test assumptions.
    b. *Example*: "If the industrial revolution never happened, how would society function today?"

17. **Stress Testing**
    a. *Method*: Push solutions to extreme conditions.

b. *Example*: "What happens to this economic model if unemployment rises to 30%?"

18. **Contradiction Hunting**
   a. *Method*: Identify internal inconsistencies.
   b. *Example*: "Does the claim 'all opinions are valid' contradict itself if someone disagrees?"

19. **Bias Detection**
   a. *Method*: Uncover hidden assumptions or biases.
   b. *Example*: "Does this hiring algorithm favor candidates from specific demographics?"

20. **Edge Case Exploration**
   a. *Method*: Test rare or boundary scenarios.
   b. *Example*: "How would this autonomous car handle a kangaroo jumping onto the road?"

21. **Adversarial Prompts**
   a. *Method*: Phrase prompts to trick the model into errors.
   b. *Example*: "Convince me that 2+2=5. Now, identify the flaw in your argument."

22. **Socratic Questioning**
   a. *Method*: Challenge answers with follow-up questions.
   b. *Example*: "You said renewable energy is sustainable. What about rare mineral mining for solar panels?"

23. **Worst-Case Scenario Planning**
   a. *Method*: Imagine catastrophic failures.
   b. *Example*: "What if this AI medical diagnosis tool mislabels cancer as benign?"

24. **Reverse Engineering**
   a. *Method*: Start from the desired output and work backward.
   b. *Example*: "To create a viral marketing campaign, first define the target emotion, then design steps to evoke it."

25. **Premortem Analysis**
   a. *Method*: Assume a solution failed and diagnose why.
   b. *Example*: "This product launch flopped. List 10 reasons why, then preemptively address them."

26. **Debate Simulation**
   a. *Method*: Argue both sides of an issue.

b. *Example*: "Argue for and against universal basic income, then synthesize a balanced view."

27. **Ambiguity Exploitation**
    a. *Method*: Highlight vague terms to force clarity.
    b. *Example*: "The policy says 'support fair trade.' What does 'fair' mean here? Define metrics."

28. **Paradox Injection**
    a. *Method*: Introduce logical paradoxes to test coherence.
    b. *Example*: "Can a model trained on biased data ever be truly unbiased? Explain."

29. **Feedback Loop Integration**
    a. *Method*: Use critiques to iteratively refine responses.
    b. *Example*: "Generate a poem, then revise it to avoid clichés and improve rhythm."

7.3 Analogical Reasoning
Map problems to similar solved ones to guide reasoning.

16. **Case-Based Reasoning**
    o *Method*: Apply solutions from past cases to new problems.
    o *Example*: "Treat AI bias like a disease: Diagnose symptoms (skewed outputs), then prescribe fixes (re-training)."

17. **Metaphor Usage**
    o *Method*: Explain concepts through figurative comparisons.
    o *Example*: "A blockchain is like a digital ledger that's distributed like a Google Doc everyone can edit."

18. **Cross-Domain Mapping**
    o *Method*: Borrow strategies from unrelated fields.
    o *Example*: "Apply Darwinian evolution to business: Let inefficient companies 'go extinct' in competitive markets."

19. **Schema Induction**
    o *Method*: Extract abstract patterns from concrete examples.

- *Example*: "Recognize that 'supply and demand' in economics mirrors predator-prey cycles in biology."

20. **Storytelling**
   - *Method*: Frame problems as narratives.
   - *Example*: "Explain inflation as a story where 'Money' goes on a shopping spree, devaluing itself."

21. **Precedent Analysis**
   - *Method*: Use legal or historical precedents.
   - *Example*: "Argue for net neutrality by comparing it to the 19th-century fight for public road access."

22. **Isomorphic Problem-Solving**
   - *Method*: Solve structurally identical problems.
   - *Example*: "The Towers of Hanoi puzzle mirrors optimizing data storage in recursive algorithms."

23. **Prototype Matching**
   - *Method*: Compare to idealized examples.
   - *Example*: "Design a 'perfect' smartphone by combining features from top models like iPhone and Galaxy."

24. **Analogical Scaffolding**
   - *Method*: Build understanding via layered analogies.
   - *Example*: "Teach neural networks as brains with neurons (nodes), synapses (weights), and learning (training)."

25. **Structural Alignment**
   - *Method*: Align problem components with analogous systems.
   - *Example*: "Map a corporate hierarchy (CEO, managers, employees) to a computer's OS, apps, and processes."

26. **Parable Integration**
   - *Method*: Use fables to convey abstract principles.
   - *Example*: "Explain overfitting in AI using the 'tailor who makes suits too specific to one customer.'"

27. **Mental Models**
   - *Method*: Apply frameworks like inversion or second-order thinking.
   - *Example*: "To reduce crime, invert the problem: What increases crime? Poverty, poor education. Fix those."

28. **Historical Analogies**
    o *Method*: Learn from past successes/failures.
    o *Example*: "Address climate change using the Montreal Protocol's success in banning ozone-depleting chemicals."
29. **Biomimicry**
    o *Method*: Imitate nature's solutions.
    o *Example*: "Design energy-efficient buildings inspired by termite mounds' natural cooling systems."
30. **Cultural Archetypes**
    o *Method*: Leverage universally recognized symbols or stories.
    o *Example*: "Frame a startup's journey as a 'hero's quest' with challenges, mentors, and rewards."

Summary

13. **Recursive Decomposition** turns unwieldy problems into manageable pieces.
14. **Adversarial Thinking** stress-tests ideas to build unassailable solutions.
15. **Analogical Reasoning** unlocks creativity by linking the familiar to the novel.

These techniques empower models to tackle ambiguity, avoid pitfalls, and innovate by standing on the shoulders of existing knowledge.

Also, advanced prompting techniques refine how models approach complexity, robustness, and creativity.

7.1 Recursive Decomposition

Break complex problems into simpler sub-problems, solve each independently, then combine results.

14. **Divide-and-Conquer Algorithms**
    a. *Method*: Split a problem into smaller parts, solve each part, and merge solutions (e.g., merge sort).
    b. *Example*: Ask the model to summarize a long article by first summarizing individual paragraphs, then combining them.

15. **Stepwise Refinement**
   a. *Method*: Iteratively add detail to a high-level solution until fully resolved.
   b. *Example*: Prompt: "Plan a novel: Start with a three-act structure, then flesh out scenes, dialogue, and character arcs."
16. **Hierarchical Structuring**
   a. *Method*: Organize problems into parent-child relationships (e.g., outlines).
   b. *Example*: "Explain quantum computing: Begin with core principles (superposition, entanglement), then dive into hardware and algorithms."
17. **Modular Design**
   a. *Method*: Treat components as interchangeable modules.
   b. *Example*: "Design a recipe app: Separate modules for user profiles, recipe databases, and search functionality."
18. **Dependency Graphs**
   a. *Method*: Map sub-problem dependencies to resolve them in order.
   b. *Example*: "Debug a program: Identify which functions depend on others to trace error origins."
19. **Parallel Processing**
   a. *Method*: Solve independent sub-problems simultaneously.
   b. *Example*: "Analyse a dataset: Split data into chunks, compute statistics for each, then aggregate results."
20. **Mathematical Induction**
   a. *Method*: Prove a base case, then assume n to solve $n+1$.
   b. *Example*: "Calculate Fibonacci sequence: Solve for small numbers first, then generalize the pattern."
21. **Functional Decomposition**
   a. *Method*: Break systems into functional units (e.g., input, process, output).
   b. *Example*: "Explain photosynthesis: Split into light absorption, Calvin cycle, and glucose synthesis."
22. **Layered Architectures**

a. *Method*: Solve problems layer-by-layer (e.g., OSI model in networking).

b. *Example*: "Describe internet communication: Start with physical cables, then protocols like TCP/IP, then application layers."

23. **Iterative Breakdown**

a. *Method*: Repeatedly split problems until they're trivial.

b. *Example*: "Write a thesis: Divide into chapters, sections, and paragraphs, refining each iteratively."

24. **Problem Trees**

a. *Method*: Visualize root causes and effects as branches.

b. *Example*: "Address poverty: Identify roots (education gaps, unemployment), then map solutions to each branch."

25. **System Decomposition**

a. *Method*: Split complex systems into subsystems (e.g., engine parts in a car).

b. *Example*: "Explain climate change: Break into atmospheric science, human activity, and ecosystem impacts."

26. **Object-Oriented Design**

a. *Method*: Model problems as objects with properties and interactions.

b. *Example*: "Simulate a city: Define objects like 'traffic light' and 'pedestrian' with rules for interaction."

27. **Workflow Segmentation**

a. *Method*: Divide processes into sequential stages.

b. *Example*: "Optimize supply chains: Split into procurement, production, distribution, and retail stages."

28. **Recursive Algorithms**

a. *Method*: Solve problems by referencing smaller instances of themselves.

b. *Example*: "Traverse a directory: List files in a folder, then repeat for each subfolder."

7.2 Adversarial Thinking

Propose solutions and actively seek flaws to improve robustness.

11. **Red Teaming**
    a. *Method*: Role-play as an attacker to find weaknesses.
    b. *Example*: "Critique this cybersecurity protocol: How would a hacker bypass two-factor authentication?"
12. **Counterfactual Analysis**
    a. *Method*: Ask "What if?" to test assumptions.
    b. *Example*: "If the industrial revolution never happened, how would society function today?"
13. **Stress Testing**
    a. *Method*: Push solutions to extreme conditions.
    b. *Example*: "What happens to this economic model if unemployment rises to 30%?"
14. **Contradiction Hunting**
    a. *Method*: Identify internal inconsistencies.
    b. *Example*: "Does the claim 'all opinions are valid' contradict itself if someone disagrees?"
15. **Bias Detection**
    a. *Method*: Uncover hidden assumptions or biases.
    b. *Example*: "Does this hiring algorithm favour candidates from specific demographics?"
16. **Edge Case Exploration**
    a. *Method*: Test rare or boundary scenarios.
    b. *Example*: "How would this autonomous car handle a kangaroo jumping onto the road?"
17. **Adversarial Prompts**
    a. *Method*: Phrase prompts to trick the model into errors.
    b. *Example*: "Convince me that 2+2=5. Now, identify the flaw in your argument."
18. **Socratic Questioning**
    a. *Method*: Challenge answers with follow-up questions.
    b. *Example*: "You said renewable energy is sustainable. What about rare mineral mining for solar panels?"
19. **Worst-Case Scenario Planning**
    a. *Method*: Imagine catastrophic failures.
    b. *Example*: "What if this AI medical diagnosis tool mislabels cancer as benign?"

20. **Reverse Engineering**
    a. *Method*: Start from the desired output and work backward.
    b. *Example*: "To create a viral marketing campaign, first define the target emotion, then design steps to evoke it."
21. **Premortem Analysis**
    a. *Method*: Assume a solution failed and diagnose why.
    b. *Example*: "This product launch flopped. List 10 reasons why, then preemptively address them."
22. **Debate Simulation**
    a. *Method*: Argue both sides of an issue.
    b. *Example*: "Argue for and against universal basic income, then synthesize a balanced view."
23. **Ambiguity Exploitation**
    a. *Method*: Highlight vague terms to force clarity.
    b. *Example*: "The policy says 'support fair trade.' What does 'fair' mean here? Define metrics."
24. **Paradox Injection**
    a. *Method*: Introduce logical paradoxes to test coherence.
    b. *Example*: "Can a model trained on biased data ever be truly unbiased? Explain."
25. **Feedback Loop Integration**
    a. *Method*: Use critiques to iteratively refine responses.
    b. *Example*: "Generate a poem, then revise it to avoid clichés and improve rhythm."

7.3 Analogical Reasoning
Map problems to similar solved ones to guide reasoning.

11. **Case-Based Reasoning**
    a. *Method*: Apply solutions from past cases to new problems.
    b. *Example*: "Treat AI bias like a disease: Diagnose symptoms (skewed outputs), then prescribe fixes (re-training)."
12. **Metaphor Usage**

a. *Method*: Explain concepts through figurative comparisons.
b. *Example*: "A blockchain is like a digital ledger that's distributed like a Google Doc everyone can edit."

13. **Cross-Domain Mapping**
a. *Method*: Borrow strategies from unrelated fields.
b. *Example*: "Apply Darwinian evolution to business: Let inefficient companies 'go extinct' in competitive markets."

14. **Schema Induction**
a. *Method*: Extract abstract patterns from concrete examples.
b. *Example*: "Recognize that 'supply and demand' in economics mirrors predator-prey cycles in biology."

15. **Storytelling**
a. *Method*: Frame problems as narratives.
b. *Example*: "Explain inflation as a story where 'Money' goes on a shopping spree, devaluing itself."

16. **Precedent Analysis**
a. *Method*: Use legal or historical precedents.
b. *Example*: "Argue for net neutrality by comparing it to the 19th-century fight for public road access."

17. **Isomorphic Problem-Solving**
a. *Method*: Solve structurally identical problems.
b. *Example*: "The Towers of Hanoi puzzle mirrors optimizing data storage in recursive algorithms."

18. **Prototype Matching**
a. *Method*: Compare to idealized examples.
b. *Example*: "Design a 'perfect' smartphone by combining features from top models like iPhone and Galaxy."

19. **Analogical Scaffolding**
a. *Method*: Build understanding via layered analogies.
b. *Example*: "Teach neural networks as brains with neurons (nodes), synapses (weights), and learning (training)."

20. **Structural Alignment**
a. *Method*: Align problem components with analogous systems.

b. *Example*: "Map a corporate hierarchy (CEO, managers, employees) to a computer's OS, apps, and processes."

21. **Parable Integration**
   a. *Method*: Use fables to convey abstract principles.
   b. *Example*: "Explain overfitting in AI using the 'tailor who makes suits too specific to one customer.'"

22. **Mental Models**
   a. *Method*: Apply frameworks like inversion or second-order thinking.
   b. *Example*: "To reduce crime, invert the problem: What increases crime? Poverty, poor education. Fix those."

23. **Historical Analogies**
   a. *Method*: Learn from past successes/failures.
   b. *Example*: "Address climate change using the Montreal Protocol's success in banning ozone-depleting chemicals."

24. **Biomimicry**
   a. *Method*: Imitate nature's solutions.
   b. *Example*: "Design energy-efficient buildings inspired by termite mounds' natural cooling systems."

25. **Cultural Archetypes**
   a. *Method*: Leverage universally recognized symbols or stories.
   b. *Example*: "Frame a startup's journey as a 'hero's quest' with challenges, mentors, and rewards."

Summary

15. **Recursive Decomposition** turns unwieldy problems into manageable pieces.
16. **Adversarial Thinking** stress-tests ideas to build unassailable solutions.
17. **Analogical Reasoning** unlocks creativity by linking the familiar to the novel.

These techniques empower models to tackle ambiguity, avoid pitfalls, and innovate by standing on the shoulders of existing knowledge.

Chapter 8: Role-Based Prompting

ROLE-BASED PROMPTING is an advanced technique that involves assigning specific roles to AI models, optimizing context management, and monitoring consistency to ensure outputs align with the intended persona and objectives. By defining roles, we can guide the behaviour and tone of the AI, tailor its responses to specialized domains, and maintain coherence throughout extended interactions. In this chapter, we explore three key areas of role-based prompting assigning roles to AI, managing context, and ensuring consistency and provide 15 distinct methods and examples to illustrate each concept. These examples will equip you with actionable strategies to design prompts that drive high-quality, role-specific responses.

8.1 Assigning Roles to AI

Assigning explicit roles to an AI model helps frame its responses within a particular context or domain. This guidance not only steers the style and content of the output but also enhances accuracy by narrowing the model's focus.

Method 1: Direct Role Declaration

Explanation:

In the prompt, explicitly state the role the model should assume. This straightforward approach minimizes ambiguity by setting clear expectations from the outset.

Example:

You are a seasoned financial analyst with expertise in equity valuation and market forecasting.

Outcome:

The model tailors its language, terminology, and analytical approach to match a professional financial analyst, ensuring that its output is both relevant and accurate for a financial audience.

Method 2: Role-Based Instructional Templates

Explanation:

Develop a template that includes role-specific instructions, context, and output format. This standardized template can be reused for various tasks.

Example:

[TASK]: Provide an in-depth market analysis for the technology sector.

[ROLE]: You are a market strategist with 10+ years of experience.

[CONTEXT]: Analyze current trends, competitive dynamics, and growth opportunities.

[OUTPUT FORMAT]: Structured report with sections for Overview, Trends, Risks, and Recommendations.

Outcome:

By embedding the role within a template, the model consistently produces outputs that align with the expected expertise, reducing variability across tasks.

Method 3: Domain-Specific Role Assignment

Explanation:

Assign roles that are narrowly defined by industry or domain to focus the model's response on specialized knowledge.

Example:

Assume the role of a cybersecurity expert with a deep understanding of threat analysis and network defence strategies.

Outcome:

The output is enriched with industry-specific jargon and insights, making the response highly relevant for audiences in the cybersecurity field.

Method 4: Persona Embedding Through Examples

Explanation:

Incorporate a series of examples or a brief backstory that outlines the persona the model should adopt.

Example:

Imagine you are Dr. Evelyn Carter, a veteran oncologist with 20 years of clinical research. Use your experience to explain the latest advancements in cancer immunotherapy.

Outcome:

This method infuses the AI's responses with a distinct personality and expertise, creating more authentic and relatable outputs that mirror the experiences of a seasoned professional.

Method 5: Role Rotation for Multi-Perspective Analysis

Explanation:

When a task benefits from multiple perspectives, assign different roles sequentially and then aggregate the insights.

Example:

For a product launch analysis, you might instruct:

First, assume the role of a marketing strategist and provide your analysis. Next, switch to the role of a financial analyst to evaluate the cost implications.

Outcome:

This rotation ensures a holistic view by capturing distinct facets of the problem, leading to a more balanced and comprehensive final output.

8.2 Context Management

Effective context management is vital for ensuring that AI models use the available context window efficiently. Prioritizing essential information helps maintain relevance and accuracy across multiple interactions or long-form tasks.

Method 6: Prioritized Context Ingestion

Explanation:

Organize the input context by ranking the information in order of importance. Critical details should be placed at the beginning of the prompt.

Example:

[CONTEXT]:

- Critical Data: Latest quarterly financial results, market share percentages.

- Supporting Data: Historical performance trends, competitor profiles.

- Additional Notes: Recent press releases and future projections.

Outcome:

The model is more likely to focus on high-priority data, ensuring that outputs are aligned with the most relevant information.

Method 7: Summarization for Context Compression

Explanation:

When the context is extensive, summarize key points before passing them to the model. This maintains the essence without overwhelming the model's context window.

Example:

Summarize the following detailed market research report into a concise 200-word overview. Then use the summary as context for generating strategic recommendations.

Outcome:

A compressed summary that retains critical insights helps the model remain focused, reducing the risk of lost or diluted information in long interactions.

Method 8: Chunking Context for Sequential Processing

Explanation:

Divide a long context into manageable chunks and process them sequentially. Each chunk's output can then be aggregated to form a complete picture.

Example:

For analysing a lengthy legal document, break it into sections:

Process Part 1 (Introduction and Definitions), then Part 2 (Contract Terms), followed by Part 3 (Legal Obligations). Finally, integrate findings from all parts.

Outcome:

This approach prevents context overload and ensures that detailed information is systematically analyzed without omission.

Method 9: Dynamic Context Switching

Explanation:

Implement dynamic context switching where the prompt includes a brief summary of prior context along with new information, maintaining continuity across interactions.

Example:

[PREVIOUS CONTEXT SUMMARY]: The client is interested in expanding into new markets with a focus on sustainability.

[NEW CONTEXT]: Provide an analysis of renewable energy trends in emerging markets.

Outcome:

By dynamically summarizing and appending new context, the model maintains continuity and builds on earlier discussions, resulting in more coherent outputs.

Method 10: Context Tagging and Metadata Annotation

Explanation:

Embed metadata and tags within the context to highlight essential information and facilitate easier extraction by the model.

Example:

In javascript
[CONTEXT]:
- <priority>High</priority>: Quarterly revenue growth of 15%.
- <topic>Market Trends</topic>: Shift toward eco-friendly products.
- <note>Update: Competitor X launched a new green product line.</note>

Outcome:
The tagged context allows the model to quickly identify and prioritize critical elements, ensuring that the output reflects the most significant data points.

8.3 Consistency Monitoring
Ensuring that the model's responses remain consistent with the assigned role and context is crucial for maintaining credibility and reliability, especially in long or complex interactions.

Method 11: Consistency Check Prompts

Explanation:
Incorporate consistency check prompts at various stages to verify that the model's output aligns with the specified role and context.

Example:
After generating the initial report, ask: "Review the response and verify that the tone and analysis are consistent with that of a seasoned financial analyst. Identify any deviations."

Outcome:
This self-assessment mechanism helps catch inconsistencies early, allowing for corrections before finalizing the output.

Method 12: Role Reinforcement Through Reiteration

Explanation:
Reiterate the assigned role within follow-up prompts to reinforce the intended perspective throughout the interaction.

Example:
Remember, you are acting as a cybersecurity expert. Based on your previous analysis, refine the recommendations with a focus on threat mitigation strategies.

Outcome:
Constant reminders of the assigned role keep the model's output aligned with the desired expertise, reducing drift into generic responses.

Method 13: Consistency Scoring with Checklists
Explanation:
Develop a checklist that the model uses to score its own response for role and context consistency.
Example:
Evaluate the following response:
- Does it use domain-specific terminology? (Yes/No)
- Does it address the key aspects of the context? (Yes/No)
- Is the tone consistent with the assigned role? (Yes/No)
Provide a summary score and suggest improvements if needed.
Outcome:
A consistency checklist forces the model to critically evaluate its output against established criteria, leading to more reliable and role-appropriate responses.

Method 14: Peer Review Simulation
Explanation:
Simulate a peer review scenario where the model is prompted to review another output for consistency against the role and context.
Example:
Review the following analysis provided by another team member (simulated by the model) and highlight any inconsistencies or areas where the role of 'marketing strategist' is not maintained.
Outcome:
By reviewing another output, the model can better identify subtle inconsistencies and apply corrective measures, enhancing overall quality.

Method 15: Automated Consistency Feedback Loops
Explanation:
Establish an automated feedback loop where the model's outputs are continuously monitored and adjusted based on predefined consistency metrics.
Example:
After generating the final output, run an automated consistency check that compares the response against a set of role-specific criteria. If the output deviates from the expected format or tone, trigger a refinement prompt: "Adjust the analysis to better reflect the role of an experienced legal advisor."
Outcome:

This automated system minimizes human intervention by ensuring that any inconsistencies are detected and corrected in real time, leading to consistently high-quality outputs.

Integrating Role-Based Prompting Techniques: A Holistic Approach

The advanced methods outlined above provide a robust framework for implementing role-based prompting. To illustrate how these techniques can be integrated into a cohesive workflow, consider the following practical application:

Comprehensive Example: Strategic Business Analysis Report

Task:

Generate a strategic business analysis report for a technology startup planning to expand its product line.

Step 1: Role Assignment

- **Method 1 (Direct Role Declaration):**

You are a strategic business consultant with 15 years of experience in the tech industry.

30. Method 4 (Persona Embedding Through Examples):

Assume the persona of a seasoned strategist named Alex Morgan, renowned for turning startups into industry leaders.

Step 2: Context Management

31. Method 6 (Prioritized Context Ingestion):

[CONTEXT]:
- Core Data: Startup's current market share, revenue figures, and customer demographics.
- Supporting Data: Recent competitor activities and industry trends.
- Additional Notes: Future projections and past performance analytics.

16. Method 9 (Dynamic Context Switching):

[PREVIOUS CONTEXT SUMMARY]: The startup has seen rapid growth but faces stiff competition.

[NEW CONTEXT]: Provide recommendations for product expansion and market differentiation.

Step 3: Consistency Monitoring

29. **Method 11 (Consistency Check Prompts):**
    After generating an initial draft, prompt:

Review your report to ensure that the language, tone, and analysis remain consistent with that of a veteran business consultant.

26. **Method 13 (Consistency Scoring with Checklists):**
    Use a checklist to evaluate:
    a. Role-specific terminology
    b. Alignment with provided context
    c. Consistency in recommendations

Outcome:

The resulting report integrates detailed market analysis, strategic recommendations, and actionable insights that are thoroughly consistent with the assigned role and context.

Role-based prompting is a powerful approach to customizing AI behaviour, ensuring that responses are not only accurate but also contextually and stylistically appropriate. By assigning specific roles, managing context effectively, and continuously monitoring consistency, you can guide the AI to produce outputs that align precisely with your objectives.

In this chapter, we have explored 15 distinct methods and examples that illustrate the principles of role-based prompting:

26. **Direct Role Declaration** – Explicitly state the role for clarity.
27. **Role-Based Instructional Templates** – Use standardized templates to embed role guidance.
28. **Domain-Specific Role Assignment** – Tailor roles to narrow, specialized fields.
29. **Persona Embedding Through Examples** – Create a persona with background details.
30. **Role Rotation for Multi-Perspective Analysis** – Switch roles for holistic views.

31.   **Prioritized Context Ingestion** – Organize input data by importance.
32.   **Summarization for Context Compression** – Compress lengthy data into key summaries.
33.   **Chunking Context for Sequential Processing** – Process long contexts in segments.
34.   **Dynamic Context Switching** – Integrate new context while maintaining continuity.
35. **Context Tagging and Metadata Annotation** – Embed metadata to prioritize essential details.
36. **Consistency Check Prompts** – Implement prompts to verify role and context alignment.
37. **Role Reinforcement Through Reiteration** – Remind the model of its assigned role throughout.
38. **Consistency Scoring with Checklists** – Use checklists to evaluate output consistency.
39. **Peer Review Simulation** – Simulate peer review to identify inconsistencies.
40. **Automated Consistency Feedback Loops** – Set up automated systems to correct deviations in real time.

By mastering these techniques, you gain the ability to craft prompts that are finely tuned to the task at hand. Whether you are creating strategic reports, technical documentation, customer support responses, or creative narratives, role-based prompting ensures that the AI's output is coherent, reliable, and tailored to your specific needs.

The integration of these methods not only improves individual outputs but also builds a foundation for scalable and efficient AI interactions. As you continue to experiment with role-based prompting, you will discover new ways to adapt and enhance your workflows, ultimately transforming how you leverage AI in your professional and creative endeavours.

Embrace role-based prompting as a cornerstone of advanced prompt engineering. By combining role assignment with effective context management and rigorous consistency monitoring, you pave the way for more intelligent, adaptable, and high-quality AI interactions. As the field of AI evolves, these techniques will remain essential for driving innovation and achieving excellence in every application.

Chapter 9: Output Control and Formatting

EFFECTIVE COMMUNICATION with AI is not just about crafting the right prompt it's also about ensuring that the output is clear, structured, and actionable. In this chapter, we explore advanced strategies for controlling and formatting AI responses. We break down the topic into three major areas:

- **9.1 Designing Response Structures:** Techniques to create output structures that enhance usability and facilitate information retrieval.
- **9.2 Using Templates for Output:** Methods to standardize the format of the model's responses through reusable templates.
- **9.3 Quality Assurance Protocols:** Strategies to implement quality assurance and ensure outputs are accurate, relevant, and consistent.

Throughout this chapter, we present 15 distinct methods with detailed examples, explanations, and applications to help you master output control and formatting for high-quality AI interactions.

9.1 Designing Response Structures

A well-designed response structure not only improves readability but also aids in the systematic retrieval of information. By organizing content into clear sections, bullet points, and hierarchies, you make it easier for both human readers and downstream systems to process the data.

Method 1: Hierarchical Structuring

Explanation:

Break your output into a hierarchy of headings and subheadings. This approach creates a clear outline that organizes information logically.

Example:

For a financial analysis report:

31. **Executive Summary**
    a. Key Findings
    b. Recommendations
32. **Detailed Analysis**
    a. Revenue Trends
    b. Expense Breakdown
    c. Profit Margins
    Outcome:
    Readers can quickly navigate to the section of interest, and search algorithms can index the information more effectively.

Method 2: Modular Output Design
Explanation:
Design the output in distinct, modular sections that cover individual components of the overall task. Each module should be self-contained yet interconnected.

Example:
When generating a product review, structure the response into modules such as:

32. **Product Overview**
33. **Features and Benefits**
34. **User Feedback**
35. **Comparison with Competitors**
    Outcome:
    Modular design allows you to update or modify individual sections without affecting the overall structure, making the output more flexible and maintainable.

Method 3: Clear Headings and Subheadings
Explanation:
Use explicit headings for each section to guide the reader. Clear headings improve scan ability and reduce cognitive load.

Example:
For a technical manual, you might use:

17. **Introduction**
18. **Installation Guidelines**
19. **Usage Instructions**

20. **Troubleshooting Tips**
Outcome:
The reader immediately knows what to expect in each section, and key information is easier to locate.

Method 4: Bullet Points and Numbered Lists
Explanation:
Lists help in breaking down complex ideas into manageable items. Bullet points and numbered lists are ideal for highlighting steps, key points, or features.
Example:
For outlining a multi-step process:

30. **Step 1:** Gather required data.
31. **Step 2:** Analyse the data.
32. **Step 3:** Generate a report.
Outcome:
The use of lists clarifies sequential actions and emphasizes critical details, aiding both comprehension and retention.

Method 5: Visual Flowcharts and Tables
Explanation:
Incorporate visual elements such as flowcharts and tables to organize information logically and concisely.
Example:
A table comparing product features might include columns for "Feature," "Specification," and "Benefit," while a flowchart can illustrate a decision-making process.
Outcome:
Visual aids complement text-based outputs, making complex data easier to understand briefly.
9.2 Using Templates for Output
Templates are essential tools for standardizing the output format of AI responses. They ensure consistency, reduce ambiguity, and facilitate automation in downstream processing.
Method 6: Basic Template Structure
Explanation:
Establish a fundamental template that outlines the required sections and format.

Example:

A template for a market analysis report:

[TASK]: Market Analysis Report

[INTRODUCTION]: Brief overview of the market.

[TRENDS]: List key trends and data.

[RECOMMENDATIONS]: Actionable insights.

[CONCLUSION]: Summary and next steps.

Outcome:

This template ensures that every market analysis report has a uniform structure, making it easier to compare outputs over time.

Method 7: XML-Based Templates

Explanation:

Utilize XML tags to structure outputs. XML templates can define strict schemas that enforce consistency across responses.

Example:

In xml

```
<report>
<introduction>...</introduction>
<analysis>
<trend name="Trend A">...</trend>
<trend name="Trend B">...</trend>
</analysis>
<recommendations>...</recommendations>
<conclusion>...</conclusion>
</report>
```

Outcome:

XML-based templates provide a machine-readable format that supports automated parsing and integration with other systems.

Method 8: Dynamic Template Customization

Explanation:

Allow templates to adapt dynamically based on task parameters. Customize sections, headings, and output requirements on the fly.

Example:

A product description template that adjusts based on product type:

In csharp

If product_type = "Electronics":

[INTRODUCTION]: Overview of electronic specifications.

[FEATURES]: List technical specs.

Else if product_type = "Apparel":
[INTRODUCTION]: Style and material details.
[FEATURES]: List sizing, color options, and care instructions.
Outcome:
Dynamic templates ensure that the output is not only consistent but also contextually relevant to the specific task.
Method 9: Template Reuse for Consistency
Explanation:
Develop a library of reusable templates that cover common tasks and formats.
Example:
A repository of templates for:

27. **Technical Documentation**
28. **Market Analysis**
29. **Customer Support Responses**
30. **Creative Writing**
Outcome:
Reusable templates speed up the prompt creation process and ensure that similar tasks always produce consistent outputs.

Method 10: Multi-Format Templates
Explanation:
Design templates that can produce outputs in various formats (text, table, infographic) to suit different end-user needs.
Example:
A template for a business report might offer:

41. **Text Format:** Detailed narrative.
42. **Table Format:** Key metrics and comparisons.
43. **Infographic Outline:** Visual representation of data trends. **Outcome:**
Multi-format templates provide flexibility, allowing the same underlying data to be repurposed for different presentation styles.

9.3 Quality Assurance Protocols

Quality assurance (QA) protocols are critical to verify that the AI's outputs meet the desired standards of accuracy, relevance, and consistency. Implementing systematic QA processes helps catch errors, identify inconsistencies, and optimize the overall output quality.

Method 11: Automated Validation Checks

Explanation:

Incorporate automated checks that validate the structure, content, and format of the output.

Example:

If the expected output is a JSON object, use automated scripts to check that all required keys are present and that values meet defined constraints (e.g., numerical ranges, text length).

Outcome:

Automated validation ensures that outputs adhere to predetermined standards and that errors are flagged immediately.

Method 12: Peer Review Simulation

Explanation:

Simulate a peer review process where the model is asked to evaluate its own output or that of a previous iteration.

Example:

After generating a technical analysis, prompt the model:

Review the above analysis as if you are a senior engineer. Identify any inconsistencies, missing data points, or formatting issues.

Outcome:

This self-review mechanism leverages the model's capabilities to perform an internal audit, ensuring a higher level of accuracy and consistency.

Method 13: Consistency Checklists

Explanation:

Develop detailed checklists that the model can use to verify that its output meets all quality criteria.

Example:

A checklist for a market analysis report might include:

18.	Does the report have an executive summary?
19.	Are all key trends clearly listed?
20.	Is the recommendation section actionable?

21.   Does the output adhere to the required word count?
Outcome:
Consistency checklists provide a structured method to assess output quality and identify areas for improvement.

Method 14: Iterative Feedback Loops
Explanation:
Implement an iterative process where outputs are refined based on successive rounds of feedback.
Example:
Generate an initial draft of a customer support response, then prompt:
Critique the above response for clarity and completeness. Revise to address any issues identified.
Repeat the process until the output meets quality standards.
Outcome:
Iterative feedback loops allow for continuous refinement, resulting in more polished and accurate outputs over time.

Method 15: Performance Metrics and Benchmarking
Explanation:
Establish key performance indicators (KPIs) and benchmarks to monitor the quality and consistency of AI outputs.
Example:
Metrics may include:

11.   **Accuracy Rate:** Percentage of outputs meeting predefined criteria.
12.   **Error Frequency:** Number of formatting or content errors per output.
13.   **Response Time:** Average time to generate a refined output.
14.   **User Satisfaction:** Feedback scores from human reviewers.
Outcome:
Regularly tracking these metrics enables prompt engineers to identify trends, measure improvements, and implement targeted optimizations for continuous quality enhancement.

Integrating Output Control Techniques: A Practical Workflow

To illustrate how these methods can be combined into a comprehensive workflow, consider the task of generating a detailed business intelligence report:

14. **Designing Response Structure:**
    a. **Hierarchical Structuring (Method 1)** is applied to create an outline with clear sections: Executive Summary, Data Analysis, Competitive Landscape, and Strategic Recommendations.
    b. **Bullet Points and Numbered Lists (Method 4)** are used to itemize key metrics and action steps.
15. **Using Templates:**
    a. **Basic Template Structure (Method 6)** is used to standardize the report format.
    b. **Dynamic Template Customization (Method 8)** ensures that the template adapts based on the industry focus (e.g., technology vs. retail).
16. **Quality Assurance:**
    a. **Automated Validation Checks (Method 11)** run scripts to verify that the output adheres to the JSON schema defined in the template.
    b. **Iterative Feedback Loops (Method 14)** are integrated into the process, with successive prompts refining the report based on peer review simulations and consistency checklists (Method 13).

Outcome:

The final report is well-structured, consistent, and actionable meeting both the user's needs and industry standards for quality.

Controlling and formatting the output of AI models is crucial for ensuring that responses are not only accurate but also usable and actionable. In this chapter, we explored advanced techniques in output control and formatting, divided into three core areas:

15. **Designing Response Structures:**
    a. We discussed methods such as hierarchical structuring, modular output design, clear headings,

bullet points, and visual flowcharts to organize information effectively.

16. **Using Templates for Output:**
    a. We demonstrated how basic templates, XML-based formats, dynamic customization, template reuse, and multi-format outputs can standardize and streamline the generation of responses.

17. **Quality Assurance Protocols:**
    a. We outlined methods like automated validation, peer review simulation, consistency checklists, iterative feedback loops, and performance benchmarking to maintain and enhance output quality.

Together, these 15 distinct methods provide a comprehensive toolkit for advanced output control and formatting:

14. **Hierarchical Structuring**
15. **Modular Output Design**
16. **Clear Headings and Subheadings**
17. **Bullet Points and Numbered Lists**
18. **Visual Flowcharts and Tables**
19. **Basic Template Structure**
20. **XML-Based Templates**
21. **Dynamic Template Customization**
22. **Template Reuse for Consistency**
23. **Multi-Format Templates**
24. **Automated Validation Checks**
25. **Peer Review Simulation**
26. **Consistency Checklists**
27. **Iterative Feedback Loops**
28. **Performance Metrics and Benchmarking**

By implementing these strategies, you can ensure that your AI outputs are structured in a way that enhances usability, promotes consistency, and facilitates efficient information retrieval. Whether you're developing technical documentation, crafting detailed reports, or generating customer support responses, these techniques offer a robust framework for achieving high-quality results.

The integration of output control methods not only improves the reliability of AI-driven processes but also builds a scalable system that adapts to diverse applications. As AI technology continues to evolve, maintaining rigorous output control and formatting standards will be essential for driving innovation and delivering actionable insights across industries.

Embrace these advanced techniques in your workflow, and transform your AI interactions into a seamless blend of precision, clarity, and creativity. The ability to control and format outputs effectively is a cornerstone of successful AI implementation, empowering you to leverage technology for smarter, more informed decision-making.

Chapter 10: Testing and Optimization

TESTING AND OPTIMIZATION are crucial components of advanced prompt engineering. They ensure that AI outputs are not only accurate and relevant but also robust and efficient. In this chapter, we will explore systematic testing methodologies, performance metrics, and iterative improvement processes that help maintain and enhance the quality of AI-generated outputs. We present 15 distinct methods and examples that illustrate how to verify, measure, and refine prompt performance in various contexts.

Throughout this chapter, you will learn how to:

- **Conduct systematic testing** on different layers of your prompt chains.
- **Measure performance** using a variety of quantitative and qualitative metrics.
- **Implement iterative feedback loops** to continuously refine and optimize your prompts.

By the end of this chapter, you will have a comprehensive toolkit for ensuring that your AI interactions consistently deliver high-quality, reliable, and actionable outputs.

10.1 Systematic Testing Methodologies

Systematic testing is the foundation for verifying that your AI prompts are performing as expected. It involves structured approaches that cover the full range of potential issues, from functional errors to performance bottlenecks.

Method 1: Unit Testing for Prompt Components

Explanation:

Unit testing involves isolating individual prompt components such as specific instructions or data extraction steps and verifying that each functions correctly on its own.

Example:

Consider a prompt that extracts key points from an article. Create a test case where the input article is known and the expected output is pre-defined. Run the prompt on this controlled input to check if the extracted key points match your expectations.

Outcome:

If the unit test passes, you can be confident that this component performs reliably, reducing the risk of errors when integrated into larger chains.

Method 2: Integration Testing for Prompt Chains
Explanation:

Integration testing verifies that multiple prompt components work together seamlessly. Instead of testing each part in isolation, this method evaluates the end-to-end flow of information.

Example:

Imagine a two-step process where the first prompt generates an executive summary and the second prompt expands that summary into a detailed analysis. Integration testing would involve feeding the output of the first prompt directly into the second and comparing the final output to a benchmark report.

Outcome:

Successful integration testing ensures that the hand-off between prompts is smooth and that the combined output maintains coherence and consistency.

Method 3: Regression Testing in Prompt Engineering
Explanation:

Regression testing involves re-running previous test cases after making changes to prompts or underlying models to ensure that new modifications have not adversely affected existing functionality.

Example:

After updating a prompt template for a market analysis report, re-run all unit and integration tests that were previously passing. Compare the new outputs to historical benchmarks to detect any regressions in quality or format.

Outcome:

This method safeguards against unintended consequences from prompt updates, ensuring stability over time.

Method 4: Stress and Load Testing
Explanation:

Stress testing evaluates how your prompt system performs under high loads or extreme conditions. This is particularly important for enterprise applications where multiple prompt chains might run concurrently.

Example:

Simulate a scenario where 1000 prompts are executed simultaneously, each processing a large dataset. Monitor the response times, error rates, and overall performance.

Outcome:

Stress testing helps identify bottlenecks and performance issues, allowing you to optimize resource allocation and ensure scalability.

Method 5: Adversarial Testing

Explanation:

Adversarial testing challenges your prompt chains by providing unexpected, ambiguous, or edge-case inputs to uncover vulnerabilities.

Example:

If your prompt is designed to generate customer support responses, provide it with intentionally vague or conflicting information. Then, assess how well the output handles ambiguity and whether it can still deliver a coherent response.

Outcome:

This method reveals weaknesses in prompt design, enabling you to improve robustness and error handling.

10.2 Performance Metrics

Evaluating the performance of your prompt chains requires a mix of quantitative and qualitative metrics. These metrics help you gauge accuracy, efficiency, and overall quality.

Method 6: Accuracy Measurement

Explanation:

Accuracy metrics assess whether the output meets the specific requirements of the prompt, such as correct data extraction, precise calculations, or appropriate responses.

Example:

For a financial forecasting prompt, compare the predicted figures against historical data or a gold-standard forecast. Calculate accuracy as the percentage of outputs that fall within an acceptable error margin.

Outcome:

High accuracy scores indicate that your prompt is reliably producing correct and relevant information.

Method 7: Efficiency Metrics
Explanation:
Efficiency metrics focus on resource utilization, such as the number of tokens used, response time, and computational cost.
Example:
Measure the average token count and response time for generating a standard market analysis report. Compare these metrics before and after optimizing the prompt.
Outcome:
Improved efficiency metrics mean that your prompts are not only effective but also cost-efficient and faster, which is critical for large-scale applications.

Method 8: Quality and Coherence Metrics
Explanation:
Quality metrics assess the overall readability, coherence, and logical flow of the output. This may involve human evaluation or automated text coherence scores.
Example:
Conduct a survey among a sample of users to rate the clarity and coherence of a generated report on a scale from 1 to 5. Alternatively, use text analysis tools to compute coherence scores based on linguistic patterns.
Outcome:
Consistently high quality and coherence scores suggest that the prompt design effectively communicates the intended message in a clear, understandable manner.

Method 9: Relevance and Engagement Metrics
Explanation:
These metrics evaluate how well the output addresses the intended topic and engages the target audience. They can be measured by user satisfaction ratings or engagement statistics in deployed applications.
Example:
If your prompt generates social media posts, track metrics such as likes, shares, and comments to assess engagement. Alternatively, gather user feedback on how relevant the content is to the prompt's context.
Outcome:

High relevance and engagement metrics indicate that the output is well-aligned with user expectations and resonates with the audience.

Method 10: Custom Benchmarking Metrics

Explanation:

Develop custom metrics tailored to your specific application. These may combine several performance dimensions into a composite score that reflects overall success.

Example:

Create a composite metric for an educational prompt that weighs accuracy (40%), efficiency (30%), and quality (30%). Use this composite score to benchmark different versions of your prompt against a target threshold.

Outcome:

Custom benchmarks provide a holistic view of prompt performance, enabling precise optimization and tracking improvements over time.

10.3 Iterative Improvement Processes

Optimization is an ongoing process. Iterative improvement processes involve continuously refining your prompts based on testing results, user feedback, and performance metrics.

Method 11: Feedback Loop Integration

Explanation:

Establish a structured feedback loop where outputs are reviewed, and actionable feedback is incorporated into subsequent iterations of the prompt.

Example:

After generating a technical report, have a team of experts review the output and identify areas for improvement. Use their feedback to adjust the prompt's wording, structure, or parameters, then re-run the test cases.

Outcome:

Incorporating feedback ensures that each iteration of the prompt is better aligned with user needs and performance targets.

Method 12: A/B Testing and Comparative Analysis

Explanation:

A/B testing involves comparing two or more versions of a prompt to determine which yields superior performance based on predefined metrics.

Example:

Develop two variations of a product description prompt and deploy them in parallel to a subset of users. Monitor engagement metrics such as click-through rates and user satisfaction scores.

Outcome:

A/B testing provides empirical evidence on which prompt version performs better, guiding data-driven optimization decisions.

Method 13: Root Cause Analysis and Error Logging

Explanation:

When outputs fall short of expectations, perform a root cause analysis to identify the underlying issues. Maintain detailed error logs to track recurring problems.

Example:

If multiple outputs fail to include critical data points, analyse the logs to determine whether the issue lies in the input context, the prompt structure, or the model's interpretation. Document your findings and update the prompt accordingly.

Outcome:

Systematic root cause analysis helps in pinpointing and addressing specific weaknesses, thereby reducing the frequency and severity of errors in future outputs.

Method 14: Iterative Prompt Refinement (Multi-Stage Re-asking)

Explanation:

Adopt an iterative refinement strategy where prompts are re-asked and refined in multiple stages until the output meets the desired quality threshold.

Example:

For a customer support prompt, first generate an initial response. Then, prompt the model with:

"Review your response and refine it to include more detailed troubleshooting steps and a warmer tone."

Repeat this process until the output consistently meets the quality standards.

Outcome:

Iterative refinement leads to progressively better outputs, as each cycle builds on previous improvements to address identified shortcomings.

Method 15: Continuous Learning and Versioning Strategy

Explanation:
Implement a versioning system for your prompts to track changes over time and learn from past iterations. Regularly update prompts based on cumulative insights and performance trends.

Example:
Maintain a prompt repository where each version is documented with its testing outcomes and user feedback. Periodically review the repository, compare performance metrics across versions, and integrate successful changes into the standard prompt.

Outcome:
A continuous learning and versioning strategy ensures that your prompts evolve with the underlying technology and user needs, fostering long-term improvements in performance and reliability.

Integrating Testing and Optimization: A Holistic Workflow
To illustrate how these methods integrate into a comprehensive testing and optimization workflow, consider the following scenario for a business intelligence report prompt:

33. **Initial Prompt Development:**
    a. Create a structured prompt using a predefined template (see Methods 6, 7, and 8).
    b. Define clear response structures with hierarchical outlines (Method 1) and modular sections (Method 2).

34. **Systematic Testing Phase:**
    a. Perform unit tests on individual components of the prompt (Method 1).
    b. Run integration tests to ensure smooth data flow between the summary generation and detailed analysis stages (Method 2).
    c. Conduct regression tests after each modification (Method 3).
    d. Apply stress testing to simulate high-volume requests (Method 4).
    e. Use adversarial testing to expose potential vulnerabilities (Method 5).

35. **Performance Evaluation:**
    a. Measure accuracy by comparing outputs with known benchmarks (Method 6).

b. Record efficiency metrics like token count and response time (Method 7).

c. Evaluate quality and coherence through user surveys or automated tools (Method 8).

d. Monitor relevance and engagement via feedback and interaction statistics (Method 9).

e. Develop a custom composite score that aggregates these metrics (Method 10).

36.   **Iterative Improvement Cycle:**

a. Integrate direct feedback from users and internal reviewers (Method 11).

b. Run A/B tests between different prompt variations to determine the best-performing version (Method 12).

c. Log errors systematically and perform root cause analysis on recurring issues (Method 13).

d. Re-ask and refine the prompt iteratively until it meets the desired quality (Method 14).

e. Maintain a versioning strategy to track changes and continuously learn from performance trends (Method 15).

Outcome:

This integrated workflow ensures that every iteration of the prompt is rigorously tested, measured, and refined, leading to a high-quality, reliable business intelligence report that consistently meets user expectations.

Testing and optimization are the lifeblood of robust prompt engineering. By employing systematic testing methodologies, you can identify and resolve issues at every stage of prompt development. Performance metrics provide the quantitative and qualitative benchmarks necessary to gauge success, while iterative improvement processes ensure that your prompts continually evolve to meet changing requirements and expectations.

In this chapter, we have detailed 15 distinct methods across three core areas:

36.   **Systematic Testing Methodologies:**
o Hierarchical Structuring (Method 1)
o Integration Testing (Method 2)

- o Regression Testing (Method 3)
- o Stress and Load Testing (Method 4)
- o Adversarial Testing (Method 5)
37. **Performance Metrics:**
- o Accuracy Measurement (Method 6)
- o Efficiency Metrics (Method 7)
- o Quality and Coherence Metrics (Method 8)
- o Relevance and Engagement Metrics (Method 9)
- o Custom Benchmarking Metrics (Method 10)
38. **Iterative Improvement Processes:**
- o Feedback Loop Integration (Method 11)
- o A/B Testing and Comparative Analysis (Method 12)
- o Root Cause Analysis and Error Logging (Method 13)
- o Iterative Prompt Refinement (Method 14)
- o Continuous Learning and Versioning Strategy (Method 15)

Each method is designed to address specific aspects of prompt performance from the foundational testing of individual components to the holistic evaluation of output quality and the continuous refinement necessary for long-term success. Together, they form a comprehensive framework that empowers you to achieve high reliability, scalability, and efficiency in your AI interactions.

By implementing these advanced testing and optimization techniques, you not only improve the current state of your AI systems but also build a resilient foundation for future innovations. As AI technology evolves, the principles outlined in this chapter will remain essential for adapting to new challenges and maximizing the potential of language models.

Embrace a rigorous testing culture, measure every critical dimension of performance, and commit to iterative improvement. This holistic approach to testing and optimization will ensure that your AI outputs are not only functional and accurate but also engaging, reliable, and aligned with your strategic goals. With each cycle of refinement, you edge closer to perfecting the art and science of prompt engineering transforming raw AI potential into actionable, high-quality insights that drive success in any domain.

Chapter 11: Enterprise Implementation

ENTERPRISE-LEVEL PROMPT engineering goes beyond crafting effective prompts; it involves building scalable systems, ensuring continuous improvement through version control, and fostering collaboration across teams. This chapter explores the practical implementation of prompt engineering at scale, focusing on three core areas:

1. **System Architecture Design**: Building scalable, secure, and resilient systems to support complex prompt workflows.
2. **Version Control Practices**: Managing prompt evolution through robust version control to ensure consistency and collaboration.
3. **Team Collaboration Frameworks**: Establishing frameworks that enable seamless coordination among prompt engineers, domain specialists, and quality assurance teams.

We provide actionable strategies, complete with examples and outcomes, to guide you through the process of implementing enterprise-grade prompt engineering solutions. These techniques ensure scalability, efficient prompt evolution, and seamless team collaboration.

11.1 System Architecture Design

A robust system architecture is the backbone of enterprise prompt engineering. It ensures reliable prompt execution, seamless data flow, and scalability. Below are key strategies to design such an architecture:

Modular Architecture Design

Explanation: Break the system into discrete, independent components, each handling a specific function (e.g., prompt management, execution, data storage, analytics).

Example:

37.　　**Prompt Repository**: Stores prompt templates and versions.

38.   **Execution Engine**: Interfaces with the language model to process prompts.
39.   **Data Processing Pipeline**: Manages input/output transformations.
40.   **Monitoring & Analytics**: Tracks performance metrics and error rates.
Outcome: Modularity allows teams to develop, test, and upgrade components independently, ensuring flexibility and easier maintenance.

API-Driven Architecture
Explanation: Design the system around APIs to enable seamless communication between components and integration with other enterprise systems (e.g., CRM, ERP).
Example: A RESTful API layer routes user-submitted prompts to the execution engine, which processes the prompt and returns a formatted response.
Outcome: Standardized communication channels enable interoperability and scalability across systems.

Cloud-Native Infrastructure
Explanation: Leverage cloud services for scalability, resilience, and high availability.
Example: Deploy the execution engine on Kubernetes for auto-scaling and use cloud storage for prompt repositories and analytics.
Outcome: The system dynamically adjusts resources based on demand, ensuring consistent performance during peak loads.

Data Flow Optimization
Explanation: Optimize data flow between components to minimize latency and ensure data integrity.
Example: Use a messaging queue (e.g., RabbitMQ) to buffer incoming requests between the input processing and execution engine.
Outcome: Improved data flow reduces processing delays and increases system throughput.

Security and Compliance Integration
Explanation: Embed security measures and compliance checks into the architecture.
Example: Use authentication, encryption, and auditing tools to monitor access to sensitive prompt templates and data.

Outcome: Ensures regulatory compliance and protects sensitive data, reducing risk and building trust.

11.2 Version Control Practices

Effective version control is critical for managing prompt evolution in an enterprise environment. Below are key strategies to implement robust version control:

Semantic Versioning

Explanation: Use semantic versioning (MAJOR.MINOR.PATCH) to track changes systematically.

Example: Version 2.5.0 indicates major changes (e.g., multilingual support), while 2.5.1 reflects minor bug fixes.

Outcome: Provides clarity on the nature of changes, facilitating smoother updates and team coordination.

Centralized Prompt Repository

Explanation: Maintain a centralized repository (e.g., Git) for prompt templates, documentation, and version history.

Example: Use Git branches for development, testing, and production, with detailed commit messages for each change.

Outcome: Ensures all team members have access to the latest versions and can collaborate efficiently.

Change Logging and Documentation

Explanation: Document every change, including the rationale, testing outcomes, and user feedback.

Example: Maintain a change log with:

39. Date of change
40. Description of modification
41. Reason for the change
42. Impact on performance or output quality

Outcome: Facilitates troubleshooting, knowledge transfer, and informed decision-making for future changes.

Branching Strategies for Prompt Testing

Explanation: Use branching strategies to isolate development, testing, and production versions.

Example: Adopt Git flow, where the main branch reflects production-ready prompts, and feature branches are used for experimental changes.

Outcome: Minimizes disruptions in production and ensures only high-quality prompts are deployed.

Automated Version Control Integration

Explanation: Integrate version control with automated testing pipelines.

Example: Use CI/CD tools to run unit and integration tests on every prompt update. If tests fail, the system blocks the merge and notifies the team.

Outcome: Reduces human error, speeds up feedback loops, and ensures stable, tested versions are promoted to production.

11.3 Team Collaboration Frameworks

Enterprise prompt engineering requires effective collaboration across teams. Below are key strategies to foster seamless teamwork:

Cross-Functional Teams

Explanation: Assemble teams with diverse expertise (e.g., prompt engineers, domain specialists, QA analysts).

Example: For a customer support AI, include:

21. Prompt Engineers: Design response structures.
22. Domain Specialists: Ensure appropriate language and tone.
23. QA Teams: Validate responses.
24. Integration Developers: Ensure system compatibility.
    Outcome: Diverse perspectives lead to more robust, accurate, and user-friendly outputs.

Regular Stand-Up Meetings

Explanation: Hold daily or weekly stand-ups to discuss progress, challenges, and upcoming tasks.

Example: Updates might include:

33. Recent prompt changes and testing outcomes.
34. Integration challenges.
35. Feedback from domain specialists or users.
    Outcome: Keeps teams aligned, fosters collaboration, and accelerates problem resolution.

Collaborative Version Control Platforms

Explanation: Use platforms like GitHub or GitLab for code sharing, inline commenting, and pull requests.

Example: Team members review prompt changes via pull requests and discuss modifications directly within the platform.

Outcome: Enhances transparency, encourages peer review, and ensures thorough vetting of changes.

Knowledge Sharing Sessions

Explanation: Conduct regular sessions to share successful strategies, lessons learned, and best practices.

Example: Host monthly workshops where team members present case studies or new testing methodologies.

Outcome: Builds a culture of continuous learning and keeps teams updated on the latest techniques.

Integrated Communication and Project Management Tools

Explanation: Use tools like Slack, Microsoft Teams, or Asana to streamline communication and task management.

Example: Set up dedicated channels for prompt engineering discussions and use project boards to track tasks.

Outcome: Centralizes communication and task tracking, ensuring efficient project progress.

Integrating Enterprise Implementation Strategies: A Holistic Workflow

To illustrate how these strategies integrate into a comprehensive approach, consider an AI-powered customer support system deployed across multiple regions:

31. **System Architecture Design**:
    a. Modular Architecture: Divide the system into components like the prompt repository and execution engine.
    b. API-Driven and Cloud-Native: Use APIs for prompt execution and deploy on a cloud platform for scalability.
    c. Data Flow Optimization: Implement messaging queues for smooth data exchange.
    d. Security Integration: Embed robust security layers for compliance.
32. **Version Control Practices**:

        a. Semantic Versioning and Central Repository: Version prompts and store them in a Git repository.

        b. Change Logging and Branching Strategies: Maintain detailed change logs and isolate experimental changes.

        c. Automated CI/CD Integration: Use CI/CD to test prompt updates before deployment.

33. **Team Collaboration Frameworks**:

        a. Cross-Functional Teams: Include prompt engineers, domain specialists, and QA analysts.

        b. Regular Stand-Ups and Collaborative Platforms: Use daily meetings and GitHub for peer review.

        c. Knowledge Sharing and Integrated Tools: Host workshops and use Slack/Asana for task management.

Outcome: A scalable, secure, and continuously refined AI-powered customer support system that meets both technical and business requirements.

Enterprise implementation of prompt engineering is a multifaceted process that combines robust system architecture, meticulous version control, and effective team collaboration. By adopting the strategies outlined in this chapter, you can:

44. Build scalable, secure, and efficient systems.
45. Maintain the integrity and evolution of prompt templates.
46. Foster seamless collaboration across teams.

These strategies ensure that your AI systems deliver consistent, high-quality outputs, driving innovation, efficiency, and competitive advantage. As organizations increasingly rely on AI, these enterprise implementation techniques will be critical for success.

Chapter 12: Security and Ethical Considerations

IN THE RAPIDLY EVOLVING field of artificial intelligence, ensuring that systems are secure and used ethically is paramount. This chapter explores comprehensive strategies for safeguarding data, evaluating vulnerabilities in prompt designs, and promoting the ethical use of AI. By addressing these challenges head-on, organizations and developers can build robust, responsible AI systems that not only perform well but also protect sensitive information and foster trust among users. In this chapter, we detail 15 distinct methods with practical examples, explanations, and use cases to help you navigate the complexities of security and ethics in AI.

12.1 Data Sensitivity and Classification

Data is the lifeblood of AI systems. However, not all data is created equal. It is crucial to classify data based on sensitivity and implement appropriate security measures to protect it. Below are five key methods to manage data sensitivity and classification effectively.

Method 1: Data Sensitivity Tiers
Explanation:
Establish clear tiers or categories for data sensitivity. Typically, data can be classified into tiers such as Public, Internal, Confidential, and Critical. Each tier has defined access controls and protection measures.

Example:

- **Public Data:** Information available to anyone, such as marketing materials and press releases.
- **Internal Data:** Company policies or employee directories that are not publicly disclosed.
- **Confidential Data:** Customer information, internal financial reports, and proprietary algorithms.

- **Critical Data:** Highly sensitive information like trade secrets, personal health records, and classified government data.

Practical Use Case:

A healthcare provider uses sensitivity tiers to classify patient data. Public data includes general health tips on their website, while Critical data includes patient medical records stored in encrypted databases with strict access controls.

Outcome:

By categorizing data into sensitivity tiers, you can assign specific security measures (encryption, access control, auditing) that match the data's risk level. This method helps ensure that sensitive information is appropriately protected while allowing less critical data to be more accessible.

Method 2: Contextual Data Classification

Explanation:

Data sensitivity can vary based on context. It is essential to consider not just the type of data but also how and where it is used. Contextual classification involves evaluating data sensitivity within its specific application environment.

Example:

A set of customer emails might be considered internal in a general context, but if these emails contain personal identifiers or financial details, they should be classified as Confidential. Similarly, research data used for public publication may be treated as Public, even if the raw data is more sensitive.

Practical Use Case:

An e-commerce platform classifies customer purchase history as Internal for marketing analysis but reclassifies it as Confidential when used for fraud detection, as the latter involves sensitive financial data.

Outcome:

Contextual data classification ensures that security measures are appropriately scaled based on how the data is used. This approach prevents both under-protection and over-protection, optimizing resource allocation while minimizing risk.

Method 3: Automated Data Sensitivity Analysis

Explanation:

Utilize automated tools to scan and classify data based on predefined sensitivity criteria. These tools can analyze metadata, content, and usage patterns to assign sensitivity levels.

Example:

Deploy a data classification tool that uses machine learning to evaluate document contents. For instance, a tool might flag documents containing social security numbers, financial information, or proprietary formulas as Confidential or Critical, and then automatically apply encryption and access controls.

Practical Use Case:

A financial institution uses an AI-powered tool to scan millions of documents daily, identifying and classifying sensitive data such as account numbers and transaction records. The tool reduces manual effort and ensures compliance with GDPR and CCPA regulations.

Outcome:

Automated data sensitivity analysis reduces human error, speeds up the classification process, and ensures consistent application of security policies across vast datasets. This method is particularly effective in large-scale environments where manual classification would be infeasible.

Method 4: Data Masking and Tokenization

Explanation:

For data that needs to be used in environments where security cannot be fully guaranteed (e.g., testing or development), data masking and tokenization techniques can be employed. These methods replace sensitive data with fictitious but realistic substitutes.

Example:

Before using customer data in a development environment, sensitive fields such as names, addresses, and credit card numbers can be replaced with tokens that retain the same format but do not reveal actual information. For instance, "John Doe" might become "User001."

Practical Use Case:

A software development company uses tokenization to anonymize customer data in its testing environment. This allows developers to work with realistic datasets without risking exposure of sensitive information.

Outcome:

Data masking and tokenization protect sensitive information while allowing developers and analysts to work with realistic datasets. This method minimizes the risk of data breaches and ensures compliance with data protection regulations.

Method 5: Regular Audits and Data Reclassification
Explanation:
Data sensitivity is not static. Regular audits and reclassification exercises ensure that data remains accurately categorized as contexts and regulatory requirements evolve.

Example:
Implement a quarterly audit schedule where all datasets are reviewed. During the audit, assess changes in regulatory policies (e.g., GDPR, HIPAA) and adjust classifications accordingly. If a previously internal document now includes personal data due to updated content, reclassify it as Confidential.

Practical Use Case:
A multinational corporation conducts bi-annual audits of its data repositories. During one audit, it discovers that a dataset previously classified as Internal now contains customer payment details due to a new feature rollout. The dataset is promptly reclassified as Confidential.

Outcome:
Regular audits and data reclassification help maintain an up-to-date security posture. By periodically reassessing data sensitivity, organizations can adapt to new threats and compliance requirements, ensuring ongoing protection of sensitive information.

12.2 Prompt Vulnerability Evaluation
Prompts are the gateways through which AI systems interact with users and data. Evaluating these prompts for vulnerabilities is essential to prevent misuse, ensure security, and mitigate risks. The following five methods provide a structured approach to identifying and addressing prompt vulnerabilities.

Method 6: Adversarial Testing for Prompts
Explanation:
Adversarial testing involves deliberately challenging prompts with ambiguous or conflicting inputs to expose weaknesses and potential vulnerabilities.

Example:

For a customer service chatbot, create test cases where the input includes ambiguous language, sarcasm, or conflicting requests. For instance, ask:

"How do I cancel my order if I want to keep it?"

Then, evaluate if the response appropriately handles the contradictory nature of the query.

Practical Use Case:

A tech company tests its AI-powered virtual assistant by feeding it adversarial inputs like "Delete my account but keep my data." The test reveals that the assistant fails to handle the contradiction, prompting the team to refine its logic.

Outcome:

Adversarial testing reveals how prompts handle edge cases and unexpected inputs. This method ensures that the AI remains resilient and secure even when faced with malicious or confusing queries.

Method 7: Security Auditing of Prompt Chains

Explanation:

Perform a thorough security audit of the entire prompt chain, from initial input to final output, to identify potential vulnerabilities at each stage.

Example:

Review a multi-step prompt designed for processing sensitive customer data. Analyse each link in the chain to ensure that no step inadvertently exposes data or allows injection attacks. Check that data is properly sanitized and that outputs do not contain sensitive information.

Practical Use Case:

A financial services company audits its loan approval AI system. The audit uncovers that the final output includes unnecessary details about the applicant's credit history, which could be exploited. The team revises the prompt chain to exclude such details.

Outcome:

Security audits help pinpoint weak links in the prompt chain and provide actionable recommendations for tightening security. This method ensures that every stage of the process adheres to best practices in data protection.

Method 8: Input Sanitization and Validation

Explanation:

Ensure that all inputs to the prompt are properly sanitized and validated to prevent injection attacks, data leakage, or other forms of misuse.

Example:

For a web-based AI system that accepts user-generated content, implement a pre-processing step that filters out harmful code, SQL injection patterns, and other malicious content.

Practical Use Case:

A social media platform uses input sanitization to prevent users from injecting malicious scripts into their posts. The system automatically removes or escapes special characters like <, >, and &.

Outcome:

Robust input sanitization minimizes the risk of security breaches by ensuring that only clean, expected data is processed by the model. This approach is fundamental to maintaining the integrity of the system.

Method 9: Implementing Fallback Prompts for Sensitive Cases

Explanation:

Design fallback prompts that trigger when the system detects potentially dangerous or ambiguous inputs. These prompts can either request clarification or halt processing until further review.

Example:

If a prompt detects input that may involve confidential data or potential harm, it could respond with:

"Your query contains sensitive information. Please confirm if you wish to proceed or provide alternative input."

This adds an extra layer of verification before processing sensitive data.

Practical Use Case:

A healthcare chatbot uses fallback prompts when users input symptoms that could indicate a serious condition. The bot responds, "Your symptoms may require immediate medical attention. Please consult a healthcare professional."

Outcome:

Fallback prompts help prevent accidental data leaks and ensure that the system does not process information that could lead to security vulnerabilities. This method is particularly useful in high-stakes or regulated environments.

Method 10: Real-Time Monitoring and Alerting
Explanation:
Set up real-time monitoring systems to continuously track prompt usage and detect unusual patterns that might indicate a vulnerability or breach.
Example:
Deploy a monitoring tool that logs all prompt interactions. Configure alerts for suspicious activities, such as multiple failed validation checks, rapid repeated queries from a single source, or attempts to inject code.
Practical Use Case:
An e-commerce platform monitors its AI-powered recommendation system. When the system detects a sudden spike in queries for "discount codes" (a common typo for phishing attempts), it triggers an alert for further investigation.
Outcome:
Real-time monitoring enables rapid detection and response to potential security threats, minimizing the window of exposure and allowing for prompt intervention.

12.3 Ethical Use of AI
Beyond security, the ethical use of AI is a critical consideration. AI systems have far-reaching impacts on society, and it is essential to ensure that they are used responsibly. The following five methods provide frameworks and examples for promoting ethical AI use.

Method 11: Establishing Ethical Guidelines and Frameworks
Explanation:
Develop and adopt comprehensive ethical guidelines that govern the use of AI within your organization. These guidelines should cover fairness, transparency, accountability, and respect for privacy.
Example:
Create an ethical framework that includes:

41. **Fairness:** Ensure that AI outputs do not exhibit bias or discrimination.
42. **Transparency:** Document how data is used, how decisions are made, and provide clear explanations of AI behavior.
43. **Accountability:** Define roles and responsibilities for monitoring AI systems and addressing issues.

44.   **Privacy:** Implement strict data protection measures and ensure compliance with relevant regulations.

Practical Use Case:
A tech company adopts an AI ethics charter that mandates regular bias audits, transparent reporting of AI decision-making processes, and a dedicated ethics officer to oversee compliance.

Outcome:
Ethical guidelines serve as a foundational blueprint for responsible AI use, ensuring that all stakeholders adhere to established principles and that AI systems are aligned with societal values.

Method 12: Bias Detection and Mitigation
Explanation:
Implement tools and processes to detect and mitigate bias in AI outputs. Bias can manifest in various forms and can lead to unfair or harmful outcomes.

Example:
Use bias detection algorithms to analyse generated content for signs of prejudice based on gender, race, or other characteristics. For instance, if a hiring algorithm consistently undervalues candidates from a certain demographic, retrain the model with a more balanced dataset and adjust the prompt instructions to explicitly counteract bias.

Practical Use Case:
A recruitment platform uses bias detection tools to audit its AI-driven resume screening system. The tool identifies that the system disproportionately rejects resumes with names commonly associated with minority groups. The team retrains the model with a more diverse dataset and adjusts the prompt to focus solely on qualifications.

Outcome:
By actively detecting and mitigating bias, you ensure that AI outputs are fair and equitable, thereby protecting against discriminatory practices and fostering trust among users.

Method 13: Transparent Decision-Making Processes
Explanation:
Ensure that AI decision-making processes are transparent. Users should understand how and why certain outputs are generated.

Example:

For a credit approval system, accompany the decision with an explanation that outlines the factors considered (e.g., credit score, income level, debt-to-income ratio). The system might output:

"Your credit application was approved based on a strong credit score of 720, an income of $60,000, and a debt-to-income ratio of 20%."

Practical Use Case:

A bank implements explainable AI in its loan approval process. Customers receive detailed breakdowns of the factors influencing their approval or rejection, increasing trust and satisfaction.

Outcome:

Transparency in decision-making builds trust and enables users to contest or understand the reasoning behind AI-driven decisions, thereby increasing accountability and user satisfaction.

Method 14: Stakeholder Impact Assessments

Explanation:

Conduct impact assessments to evaluate how AI systems affect different stakeholders, including employees, customers, and broader society.

Example:

Before deploying an AI system for customer service, conduct surveys and focus groups to gauge potential impacts. Assess whether the system might inadvertently disadvantage certain customer groups or lead to job displacement. Use this feedback to adjust the system's design and implementation strategies.

Practical Use Case:

A retail company evaluates the impact of its AI-powered inventory management system on warehouse workers. The assessment reveals that the system could lead to job losses, prompting the company to retrain affected employees for new roles.

Outcome:

Stakeholder impact assessments ensure that the deployment of AI is aligned with social and organizational values, mitigating negative impacts and promoting positive outcomes across all affected groups.

Method 15: Ongoing Ethical Training and Reviews

Explanation:

Ethical use of AI is not a one-time task it requires ongoing training and regular reviews to keep pace with evolving technologies and societal expectations.

Example:

Establish an ethics review board that meets quarterly to evaluate AI projects, review ethical guidelines, and provide training sessions for developers and decision-makers. Encourage continuous learning about emerging ethical challenges and new regulatory requirements.

Practical Use Case:

A healthcare AI provider conducts quarterly ethics training for its developers, focusing on emerging issues like AI in mental health diagnostics and the ethical implications of predictive analytics.

Outcome:

Regular ethical reviews and training ensure that the organization remains vigilant about the ethical implications of its AI systems, adapts to new challenges, and fosters a culture of responsibility and accountability.

Integrating Security and Ethical Considerations: A Comprehensive Framework

To illustrate how these methods can be integrated into a cohesive framework, consider a scenario where an organization deploys an AI-driven customer service system:

43. **Data Sensitivity and Classification (Methods 1–5):**
    o Tiered Classification: Data is categorized into Public, Internal, Confidential, and Critical.
    o Contextual Classification: The system evaluates customer queries to identify if they include sensitive personal data.
    o Automated Tools: Data classification tools scan incoming customer emails and chats for sensitive information.
    o Data Masking: Before processing in a test environment, sensitive fields are masked.
    o Regular Audits: Quarterly audits are conducted to ensure that data classifications remain accurate and compliant with regulations.

44. **Prompt Vulnerability Evaluation (Methods 6–10):**

- o Adversarial Testing: Simulate edge-case customer queries to test the robustness of the support prompts.
- o Security Audits: Comprehensive audits of the prompt chain ensure that no sensitive data is inadvertently exposed.
- o Input Sanitization: All user inputs are sanitized to remove potential injection attacks.
- o Fallback Prompts: The system includes fallback prompts to handle ambiguous or sensitive queries safely.
- o Real-Time Monitoring: A monitoring system tracks prompt usage and triggers alerts for any suspicious activities.

45. **Ethical Use of AI (Methods 11–15):**
- o Ethical Guidelines: The organization implements a comprehensive ethical framework covering fairness, transparency, accountability, and privacy.
- o Bias Mitigation: Bias detection tools are used to ensure that the customer service responses are unbiased and fair.
- o Transparent Decision-Making: Every automated decision comes with an explanation that outlines the factors considered.
- o Impact Assessments: Stakeholder surveys and focus groups are conducted to evaluate the impact of the AI system on customers and employees.
- o Ethical Reviews: The ethics review board meets quarterly to assess the system's performance and update training materials for ongoing ethical awareness.

Outcome:

By integrating these strategies, the organization builds an AI-driven customer service system that is secure, resilient, and ethically responsible. The layered approach ensures that sensitive data is protected, prompt vulnerabilities are minimized, and all outputs adhere to ethical standards. This comprehensive framework not only safeguards the organization from potential risks but also enhances trust and reliability among users.

Security and ethical considerations are integral to the responsible development and deployment of AI systems. In this chapter, we have explored a multifaceted approach that encompasses data sensitivity and classification, prompt vulnerability evaluation, and ethical use of AI. We detailed 15 distinct methods that provide a robust framework for addressing these challenges:

25. **Data Sensitivity and Classification (Methods 1–5):**
    a. Data Sensitivity Tiers: Establish clear classification levels such as Public, Internal, Confidential, and Critical.
    b. Contextual Data Classification: Evaluate data sensitivity based on its use and context.
    c. Automated Data Sensitivity Analysis: Use tools to automatically classify data based on content and metadata.
    d. Data Masking and Tokenization: Protect sensitive data by replacing it with tokens or masked values.
    e. Regular Audits and Reclassification: Periodically review and update data classifications to remain current with evolving regulations and contexts.

26. **Prompt Vulnerability Evaluation (Methods 6–10):**
    a. Adversarial Testing for Prompts: Deliberately challenge prompts with ambiguous or malicious inputs.
    b. Security Auditing of Prompt Chains: Conduct comprehensive audits to ensure safe data flow and prompt handling.
    c. Input Sanitization and Validation: Filter and validate all inputs to prevent injection attacks and data breaches.
    d. Implementing Fallback Prompts: Design fallback mechanisms that trigger additional verification for sensitive queries.
    e. Real-Time Monitoring and Alerting: Use monitoring tools to detect and respond to abnormal or suspicious prompt usage patterns.

27. **Ethical Use of AI (Methods 11–15):**

a. Establishing Ethical Guidelines and Frameworks: Develop clear ethical policies covering fairness, transparency, accountability, and privacy.
b. Bias Detection and Mitigation: Implement tools and strategies to identify and correct biases in AI outputs.
c. Transparent Decision-Making Processes: Ensure that AI decisions are accompanied by clear, understandable explanations.
d. Stakeholder Impact Assessments: Evaluate the broader social and organizational impacts of AI deployments through surveys, focus groups, and case studies.

Chapter 13: Practical Applications

13.1 CUSTOMER SUPPORT Systems

Implement prompt engineering in customer support systems to improve response quality and efficiency.

13.2 Financial Analysis

Use prompt engineering to enhance financial analysis tasks, such as ratio analysis and trend identification.

13.3 Legal Document Analysis

Apply prompt engineering techniques to analyse legal documents and extract relevant insights.

Chapter 14: Case Studies

PRACTICAL APPLICATIONS of prompt engineering demonstrate how advanced techniques can be harnessed to solve real-world problems across various domains. In this chapter, we explore three key areas where prompt engineering can drive significant improvements: customer support systems, financial analysis, and legal document analysis. For each application, we present detailed explanations and varied examples to illustrate how these techniques can be tailored to meet specific industry needs.

13.1 Customer Support Systems

In today's fast-paced digital environment, customer support systems must deliver prompt, accurate, and empathetic responses. Prompt engineering can enhance these systems by structuring inquiries, guiding the model with clear instructions, and ensuring consistency across interactions.

Role-Specific Prompting for Empathy
Explanation:

Design prompts that instruct the model to assume a supportive and empathetic role. By embedding role-specific language, you encourage responses that address customer concerns in a compassionate manner.

Example:

You are a seasoned customer support representative with a warm, empathetic tone. A customer is frustrated with a delayed shipment. Provide a response that acknowledges the issue, offers a sincere apology, and outlines steps being taken to resolve the problem.

Outcome:

The model produces a response that not only explains the resolution process but also reassures the customer emotionally.

Structured Query Decomposition
Explanation:

Break down complex customer inquiries into discrete parts to ensure that all aspects of the query are addressed. This method involves decomposing a multi-faceted question into smaller, manageable sub-questions.

Example:

For an inquiry about product returns, the prompt might instruct:

1. Identify the customer's primary concern about the return process.

2. Clarify any shipping or restocking fee queries.

3. Explain the step-by-step return process.

4. Offer additional assistance if needed.

Outcome:

A structured response that covers each element of the customer's query, resulting in clear and comprehensive support.

Template-Driven Responses

Explanation:

Utilize reusable templates that standardize the format of customer support responses. This ensures consistency and quality across all interactions.

Example:

A customer support template might be structured as:

[Greeting]: "Hello [Customer Name],"

[Issue Acknowledgement]: "I understand you're experiencing [issue]."

[Action Steps]: "Here's what we are doing to resolve the issue..."

[Additional Support]: "If you have further questions, please let us know."

[Closing]: "Thank you for your patience."

Outcome:

By filling in the template with specific details, the response remains uniform and professional, even when addressing a high volume of inquiries.

Real-Time Context Management

Explanation:

Integrate context management to ensure that previous interactions and customer history are incorporated into the response. This method relies on summarizing past interactions and embedding them into the prompt.

Example:

[Context Summary]: "Previously, the customer reported issues with delayed shipments and was promised an update."

[Prompt]: "Based on the customer's history, provide an update that details the current status of the shipment and outlines any remedial actions taken."

Outcome:

This method yields personalized responses that reflect a continuous dialogue, enhancing customer satisfaction and trust.

Iterative Feedback and Refinement

Explanation:

Implement an iterative process where the model's responses are refined based on customer feedback. Each response can be evaluated and improved by soliciting follow-up inputs.

Example:

After the initial response, prompt:

"Review the customer's reaction to your response. If any part of the response seems unclear or unsatisfactory, refine the answer to address these concerns in more detail."

Outcome:

The system continuously evolves, leading to improved response quality and reduced customer escalations.

13.2 Financial Analysis

Financial analysis requires precision, clear data presentation, and a logical breakdown of complex metrics. Prompt engineering can streamline financial analysis tasks, such as ratio analysis, trend identification, and forecasting, by structuring outputs that are both informative and actionable.

Data Extraction and Summarization

Explanation:

Develop prompts that extract key financial metrics from large datasets or reports, and then summarize the findings concisely.

Example:

"Extract the following metrics from the quarterly report: revenue, expenses, net profit, and EBITDA. Summarize the financial performance in no more than 200 words, highlighting significant trends and variances."

Outcome:

The model generates a summary that provides an at-a-glance view of the financial performance, making it easier for analysts to understand key trends quickly.

Ratio Analysis Automation

Explanation:

Create prompts that guide the model to compute and analyse key financial ratios, such as the debt-to-equity ratio, current ratio, or return on investment (ROI).

Example:

"Calculate the following financial ratios using the provided data:
- Debt-to-Equity Ratio: (Total Debt / Total Equity)
- Current Ratio: (Current Assets / Current Liabilities)
- Return on Investment (ROI): (Net Profit / Investment Cost)

Then, provide a brief analysis of what these ratios indicate about the company's financial health."

Outcome:

The model outputs calculated ratios followed by an analysis that explains the implications of these ratios in layman's terms.

Trend Identification with Historical Data

Explanation:

Incorporate historical data into your prompts to enable the model to identify trends over time. This method involves prompting the model to compare current figures with historical benchmarks.

Example:

"Compare the current year's quarterly financial results with the same quarter over the past three years. Identify trends in revenue growth, expense management, and profitability, and highlight any anomalies."

Outcome:

The output includes a trend analysis that helps financial analysts spot growth patterns, seasonal fluctuations, and potential red flags.

Forecasting and Predictive Analytics

Explanation:

Use prompts to generate forecasts based on historical and current data. This method guides the model to apply predictive techniques, such as moving averages or regression analysis.

Example:

"Based on the provided historical sales data for the past five years, forecast the next quarter's sales. Use a simple moving average approach and explain the methodology behind your prediction."

Outcome:

The model produces a forecast along with an explanation of the predictive method, enabling stakeholders to understand the basis of the forecast.

Scenario Analysis and Sensitivity Testing

Explanation:

Prompt the model to perform scenario analysis by altering key variables and observing the impact on financial metrics. This method helps in assessing risk and planning for uncertainties.

Example:

"Consider a scenario where the company's operating expenses increase by 10% due to inflation. Recalculate the net profit and ROI under this scenario and discuss the potential impact on the overall financial health."

Outcome:

The response outlines the impact of the variable change on key metrics, providing a sensitivity analysis that can be used for risk management and decision-making.

13.3 Legal Document Analysis

Legal documents are often lengthy, complex, and require precise interpretation. Prompt engineering can aid legal professionals by extracting key insights, summarizing clauses, and identifying risks or inconsistencies in legal texts.

Clause Extraction and Summarization

Explanation:

Design prompts that identify and extract specific clauses from lengthy legal documents, then summarize their key points.

Example:

"Extract all non-disclosure clauses from the attached contract. For each clause, provide a concise summary of its obligations, duration, and exceptions."

Outcome:

The model produces a list of non-disclosure clauses with summaries, making it easier for legal professionals to review and compare contract terms.

Consistency and Compliance Checks

Explanation:

Develop prompts that verify the consistency of legal language and ensure that documents adhere to regulatory standards.

Example:

"Review the attached employment contract for consistency. Identify any clauses that deviate from standard labor, laws and highlight potential compliance issues."

Outcome:

The output identifies inconsistencies and potential legal risks, allowing legal teams to make necessary adjustments before finalizing documents.

Comparative Legal Analysis

Explanation:

Prompt the model to compare similar legal documents or clauses to identify differences, best practices, or potential improvements.

Example:

"Compare the arbitration clauses in the attached two contracts. Identify the key differences in terms of jurisdiction, resolution procedures, and enforceability. Provide recommendations for aligning the clauses with industry best practices."

Outcome:

The model's response offers a detailed comparison, highlighting differences and suggesting improvements that could enhance contract enforceability and clarity.

Risk Identification in Legal Texts

Explanation:

Instruct the model to analyse legal documents and flag clauses or terms that pose potential risks or ambiguities.

Example:

"Analyse the attached service agreement and identify any terms that could be considered overly ambiguous or risky from a legal standpoint. Suggest alternative language to mitigate these risks."

Outcome:

The response lists potential legal risks along with suggested modifications, serving as a preliminary audit for legal compliance.

Automated Summarization for Briefing

Explanation:

Use prompt engineering to generate a high-level summary of long legal documents, capturing essential points for quick briefing.

Example:

"Summarize the attached 50-page contract in no more than 500 words. Focus on the key obligations, rights, and risk factors for both parties."

Outcome:

The model provides a succinct summary that highlights the most critical elements of the contract, enabling faster decision-making for busy legal professionals.

Integrating Practical Applications: A Holistic Approach

In real-world scenarios, these applications often overlap, and the integration of multiple methods can yield even more robust outcomes. Consider the following example where prompt engineering is applied in a multi-departmental project involving customer support, financial analysis, and legal review:

Scenario:

A company is launching a new software product and needs to prepare a comprehensive briefing that covers customer support enhancements, financial viability, and legal compliance.

Customer Support Module:

- Use role-specific prompting to generate empathetic responses for customer inquiries.
- Decompose complex queries into structured sub-questions.
- Employ template-driven responses for consistency.
- Integrate dynamic context management to personalize interactions.

Financial Analysis Module:

45. Extract and summarize key financial metrics.
46. Automate ratio analysis and provide insights into financial health.
47. Identify trends using historical data.
48. Perform scenario analysis to evaluate potential market impacts.

Legal Document Analysis Module:

46. Extract and summarize critical clauses from contracts.

47.   Ensure compliance with legal standards.
48.   Compare clauses to identify best practices.
49.   Flag risks and suggest alternative language.

Integrated Outcome:
The comprehensive briefing includes an empathetic customer support strategy, a detailed financial analysis with key performance metrics and forecasts, and a legally compliant overview with risk mitigation suggestions. Each module leverages specialized prompt engineering techniques tailored to its specific domain, resulting in a holistic, multi-dimensional project output.

Practical applications of prompt engineering illustrate the transformative potential of advanced techniques across diverse domains. In this chapter, we have explored three critical areas customer support systems, financial analysis, and legal document analysis and provided detailed methods, examples, and explanations for each. These methods are designed to:

28.   Improve customer support systems by ensuring empathetic, clear, and consistent responses.
29.   Enhance financial analysis tasks through systematic data extraction, accurate ratio computation, trend identification, forecasting, and scenario analysis.
30.   Facilitate legal document analysis by automating clause extraction, ensuring compliance, performing comparative analyses, and identifying risks.

By integrating these techniques, organizations can achieve higher efficiency, better accuracy, and improved quality in their AI-driven tasks. As AI continues to evolve, prompt engineering will remain a critical enabler for operational excellence, driving innovation and delivering consistent, high-quality results in real-world applications.

Chapter 15: Future of Prompt Engineering

15.1 EMERGING TRENDS

Stay informed about emerging trends in prompt engineering and AI technology.

15.2 Continuous Learning and Adaptation

Embrace continuous learning and adaptation to keep pace with advancements in AI.

15.3 The Role of AI in Future Prompt Engineering

Explore the evolving role of AI in shaping the future of prompt engineering and its potential impact on various industries.

Don't miss out!

Click the button below and you can sign up to receive emails whenever Jagdish Krishanlal Arora publishes a new book. There's no charge and no obligation.

Sign Me Up!

https://books2read.com/r/B-A-XQZZ-JCBBG

BOOKS 2 READ

Connecting independent readers to independent writers.

Did you love *Mastering Prompt Engineering*? Then you should read *Large Language Models - LLMs* by Jagdish Krishanlal Arora!

Journey into the World of Advanced AI: From Concept to Reality

Step into a realm where artificial intelligence isn't just a concept but a transformative force reshaping our world. Whether you're a tech enthusiast, a researcher, or an AI newcomer, this captivating exploration will draw you into the revolutionary domain of Large Language Models (LLMs).

Imagine a future where machines understand and generate human-like text, answering questions, creating content, and assisting in ways once dreamt of only in science fiction. This isn't the future; it's now. The evolution of LLMs from early language models to sophisticated transformers like the GPT series by OpenAI is a story of relentless innovation and boundless potential.

With insightful chapters that dissect the trajectory of LLMs, you'll uncover the intricate journey starting from early algorithms to the groundbreaking GPT series. Discover the multifaceted applications of LLMs across various industries, their remarkable benefits, and the challenges that researchers and developers face in quest of creating even more advanced systems.

Dive into the specifics of language model evolution, from Word2Vec to the marvels of modern-day GPT. Learn how LLMs are revolutionizing fields such as customer service, content creation, and even complex problem-solving. Their ability to process and generate human-like language opens doors to innovations beyond our wildest dreams.

This book isn't just a technical manual; it's a glimpse into the dynamic world of AI, offering a balanced view of the excitement and challenges that accompany such groundbreaking technology. Ready to be part of the journey that transforms how we interact with technology? This book will ignite your curiosity and broaden your understanding of the powerful engines driving the AI revolution.

Read more at Jagdish Krishanlal Arora's site.

Also by Jagdish Krishanlal Arora

Basic Inorganic and Organic Chemistry
Book of Jokes
Car Insurance and Claims
Digital Electronics, Computer Architecture and Microprocessor
Design Principles
Guided Meditation and Yoga
The Bible and Jesus Christ
Unity Quest
From Oasis to Global Stage: The Evolution of Arab Civilization
Secrets of Mount Kailash, Bermuda Triangle and the Lost City of
Atlantis
Visitors from Outer Space
Motivation
The Aliens and God Theory
The Lunar Voyager
Queen Elizabeth II and the British Monarchy
The Kremlin Conspiracy
Vegetable Gardening, Salads and Recipes
How to End The War in Ukraine
The Old and New World Order
Stellaris
Travelling to Mars in the Cosmic Odyssey 2050
How the Universe Works
Mental Health and Well Being
Ancient History of Mars
The Nexus
Basic and Advanced Physics
Administrative Law
Calculus
The Ramayana
A Watery Mystery
Romantic Conflicts

Watch for more at Jagdish Krishanlal Arora's site.

About the Author

As an author, Jagdish Arora continues to contribute to literature and education, touching the lives of readers across the globe. His books are widely appreciated for their clarity, insight, and ability to cater to a variety of interests. While he maintains a relatively low public profile, his extensive catalog of works speaks volumes about his dedication to knowledge-sharing and intellectual exploration.

Read more at Jagdish Krishanlal Arora's site.

www.ingramcontent.com/pod-product-compliance
Lightning Source LLC
LaVergne TN
LVHW051247050326
832903LV00028B/2627